An amazing course, clear, powerful, brimming with information and highly recommend.
Alannah Smith

This course is perfect whether you want to dip your toe in or fully submerge yourself on your goddess journey.
Bernie Anderson

Following this comprehensive and insightful course will help you to connect with the energies of the month as well as getting to know, understand and grow closer to many different goddesses.
Sue Perryman

The Arc of the Goddess is an inspirational way to reconnect to the energies surrounding us. Following the monthly turn of the wheel is exciting and there is no right or wrong way to progress. It is a personal path of discovery, developing year after year.
Heather Dewhurst

Another wonderful Kitchen Witch course with heaps of ideas to guide you to work with the energies of each month. You start a unique journey creating your own personal pantheon of goddesses – each goddess giving you a deeper connection with her and the changing of the seasons.
Vanessa Armstrong

Arc of the
Goddess

Arc of the Goddess

Rachel Patterson
& Tracey Roberts

Winchester, UK
Washington, USA

First published by Moon Books, 2016
Moon Books is an imprint of John Hunt Publishing Ltd., Laurel House, Station Approach,
Alresford, Hants, SO24 9JH, UK
office1@jhpbooks.net
www.johnhuntpublishing.com
www.moon-books.net

For distributor details and how to order please visit the 'Ordering' section on our website.

Text copyright: Rachel Patterson & Tracey Roberts 2015

ISBN: 978 1 78535 318 5
Library of Congress Control Number: 2015956008

A CIP catalogue record for this book is available from the British Library.

Design: Stuart Davies

Printed and bound by CPI Group (UK) Ltd, Croydon, CR0 4YY, UK

We operate a distinctive and ethical publishing philosophy in all
areas of our business, from our global network of authors to
production and worldwide distribution.

CONTENTS

We would like to dedicate this book to the Kitchen Witch Coven and to all the Kitchen Witch School students. We are forever grateful for your unending support.

About the Authors

Tansy Firedragon and Sunchylde DryadMoon

High Priestesses with a combined figure of more than 30 years of experience as witches, we are total certificate tarts and have enough of them between us to wallpaper a house... We love sharing what we have learnt and our own experiences with the Craft. We have studied many areas such as Wicca, shamanic practices, druidry, herbalism, tarot, reiki, crystals, aromatherapy, all sorts of divination skills, hoodoo, progressive magic, yoga, mysteries of Avalon, historical paganism, mediumship and cake...to name a few. Our pathways are that of Kitchen Witches, we are always learning something new...and we like to laugh and eat cake...

Together we run the worldwide online Kitchen Witch School of Witchcraft and the Kitchen Witch Coven along with various other online courses working with the goddesses, gods and herbal magic along with running open rituals. We also visit moots, groups and festivals, giving talks and running workshops on witchcraft.

This book evolved from a year-long online course we designed – The Arc of the Goddess. There is also an accompanying set of Arc of the Goddess oracle cards. Details of these can be found on our website – www.kitchenwitchhearth.net.

Rachel Patterson has also written several books on the Craft, all published by Moon Books.

Bibliography:

Pagan Portals Kitchen Witchcraft
Grimoire of a Kitchen Witch
Pagan Portals Hoodoo Folk Magic
Pagan Portals Moon Magic
A Kitchen Witch's World of Magical Plants & Herbs

A Kitchen Witch's World of Magical Foods
Pagan Portals Meditation
The Art of Ritual

Your Journey Begins...

This year-long Arc of the Goddess course will take you on a personal journey of discovery, taking each month as the wheel of the year turns and introducing you to different goddesses and pantheons with your choice (or theirs...) about who you work with and how you work with them.

We hope to help you connect with the magical energies of each month as well as giving you lots of practical exercises to work with and suggestions on how to make your spiritual connection stronger.

At the end of the course we hope that not only will you have discovered your own personal pantheon of goddesses to work with, but also uncovered The Goddess Within...

The Goddess Wheel that we have created is to give you a guide, or at least a base from which to start. You don't have to stick to it, but it depicts how we see the journey of the year in goddess format.

January – Earth – Guardians of the Land
The element of earth, she is cold and dark, but she is waiting, resting and storing her energy. This is also the month when the goddesses come into their own as guardians of the land, protecting and keeping Mother Earth safe.

February – Maiden – Creatrix
She is the maiden, the creatrix of all things, and February is the month when she starts to come into her own, stirring the magical energies beneath the earth.

March – Spring – Mountains
The beginning of spring and a time of the mountain goddesses, those who bring their mountain magic to the world and the new

energies of the stirring earth.

April – Air – Bringer of the Breeze
The bringers of the breeze, those goddesses that carry the element of air and bring fresh cleansing winds of change with them.

May – Mother – Healer
She is the mother goddess, the healer and the one who nurtures Mother Earth and all that resides on her and within her.

June – Summer – Meadow
Goddesses of the meadows and the season of summer bring sunshine and happy, positive energy.

July – Fire – Keepers of the Flame
The keepers of the flame and the goddesses of the element of fire bring their passion, creativity and energy at this time.

August – Matriarch – Teacher
She is the teacher and the matriarch of goddesses, she who brings wisdom and knowledge to those who seek it.

September – Autumn – Forest
Deep in the heart of the forests are the goddesses of autumn, bringing change and transformation.

October – Water – Ladies of the Lake
The ladies of the lake and the goddesses of the watery depths bring the strength of emotion and intuition.

November – Crone – Destroyer
The goddess in her crone guise brings death and destruction, but those are necessary to clear the way for renewal and rebirth.

December – Winter – Tundra

Deep in the heart of winter are the goddesses of the tundra, helping to guide us on our inner journeys and to seek that which lies within.

You may want to work with this Goddess Wheel as you work through each month and place your own choice of goddess in each section, but you may also find that those goddesses seek you out anyway...

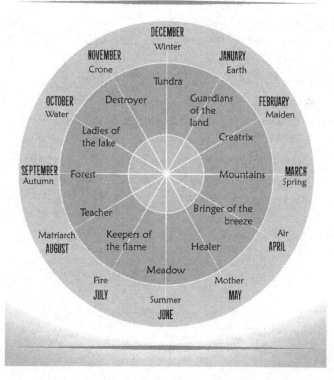

For each month we have suggested nine goddesses really just to get you started as there are many, many more that might come to you. However, as we are working with twelve months then nine goddesses for each month made sense. Why? Well...twelve times nine equals 108 and that is a pretty special number. There are 108 energy lines in the body leading to the heart chakra. It is believed that there are 108 stages to a soul's journey. Apparently the diameter of the sun is 108 times the diameter of the earth. And of course there are twelve houses in astrology and nine planets. For the nerdy maths geeks out there, when the digits of 108 are added together – 1+0+8 – it equals another magical number...nine...the number of the goddess.

There are a lot of suggestions within each lesson for practices, devotions, crafts and of course cake recipes. You can work through the lesson completing every task *or* you can cherry pick which ones suit you, you do not have to work with every single suggestion we have made. You also don't need to start in January, just jump in at whatever month it happens to be now...don't wait until the start of the year!

You may also want to keep a journal recording your thoughts and experiences throughout your journey; you can use it for whatever you want to write or not – the choice is totally yours to make.

There is no right or wrong way to work through this course, we can only guide and support you...ultimately the journey and direction is yours to take.

January

January has always been for me a bit of a damp squib month. The festivities of the Yule season have all gone, the weather is usually dark, damp, cold and dreary and everyone is suffering from over-eating and over-spending.

It is a time to withdraw, to contemplate and, okay, not actually hibernate but draw in and spend time with your inner being. Rest, recuperate, but also take some time to reflect on the year before and plot, plan and scheme for the year ahead.

Seek your inner wisdom, look for answers within and listen to your intuition and what guidance it has for you.

Deities

In this part of the course we suggest nine goddesses that we associate with this month. Have a read through the information and see if any of them resonate with you. It may be that one of them comes to you in the meditation, it might be that another deity altogether greets you...go with your intuition. We have also included a list of some deities that have celebrations or feast days within this month too.

Abundantia

Abundantia is the Roman goddess of abundance, good fortune and success. Her name means 'plenty' or 'overflowing riches'. She has also been called 'the beautiful maiden of success'. Abundantia often carries a cornucopia, known as the horn of plenty. This cornucopia is symbolic of a funnel that continually outpours from the universe, the infinite and all-encompassing supply of abundance, good fortune, opportunities, and success – constantly pouring out all good things. I definitely need to get one of these... Abundantia is extremely wise in the ways of finance. If invited she will provide guidance toward investments, finance and business/venture planning. A powerful protector of prosperity, if requested, the goddess Abundantia will safeguard valuables, providing peace of mind by ensuring that which we deem to be valuable is secure and well protected.

Don

This is a Welsh mother goddess (the equivalent of the Irish Dana). Don is an earth goddess and mother of the gods. This goddess is family personified and she brings trust along with nourishment for the earth as a whole. All her children are good and wholesome and bring light with them as they battle against darkness.

Erce

She is an Anglo Saxon goddess of the earth and known as 'Earth as Lady'. Erce is the female representation of the wheel of the year and the changes of the seasons. Worshipped as the triple goddess, her name can also be used as an invocation to the earth.

Lakshmi

Lakshmi is the Hindu goddess of light, beauty, good fortune, prosperity and wealth in both the spiritual and material realms. She rules prosperity in all forms and widely bestows her gifts on those who are open to receive it. Being the consort of Vishnu, the preserving principle, Lakshmi also signifies love and grace. Full moons are sacred to her.

White Buffalo Calf Woman

White Buffalo Calf Woman is a mother goddess of Native America. She taught the people how to survive by working with the land and growing crops as well as teaching them about sacred ceremonies and rites. She is often seen in buffalo form, offering herself up to the tribe so that they may be nourished, live and prosper.

Gaia

The Greek Mother Earth goddess, she is the beginning of all life and creation and represents all that has been created and all that grows upon the earth including all land, sky and sea. She is the lush green land and the fertile soils.

Devi

The great goddess and the ultimate female force in Hinduism, Devi's name literally means 'goddess'. She is the balance between dark and light, good and evil, and she is the mother of the entire universe. Devi is at the centre of every Hindu goddess.

Pachamama

An earth goddess from the Inca culture she rules the earth and agriculture, depicted as a dragon that sleeps under the mountains of Peru. If not honoured she sends earthquakes. If kept happy she ensures an abundance of good harvests.

Sheela Na Gig

A lusty Irish hag goddess, her carvings are found throughout Ireland as a naked female holding open her vulva. She is a dark crone goddess, guardian of all things feminine as well as the cycle of birth, death and rebirth.

Feast/Celebration Days

We have listed here the feast and celebration days for deities (we have included gods as well as goddesses) throughout January from various cultures and pantheons. These are taken from our own research...we apologise for any errors, but history is a fickle thing and calendars have changed over the years...

1st January

A Roman festival where vows were offered to Juno and Janus, presents were exchanged as a token of friendship. Dates, figs and honey were sealed in white jars and offered to Janus.

The Goddess: A Guatemalan festival where the water from five sacred coconuts is drunk and used to fertilise the ground. Women officiate the ceremony and guard the coconuts overnight, then dedicate them to the goddess before the coconut milk is drunk.

Fortuna: A Roman day of sacrifices, which were given to Fortuna to bring a year of luck and abundance.

2nd January

Isis: Offerings were made to celebrate the coming of Isis from Phoenicia.

Inanna: A white candle was lit the previous night at sunset to burn throughout the night and extinguished the next morning to celebrate the birth of Inanna.

5th January

Kore/Persephone: People spent the night in a temple singing to Alexandria, after which a statue, a wooden idol, was brought into the inner temple and carried around seven times in honour of the story of Persephone.

6th January

Ancient Italian festival of La Befana: An old hag figure, Befana flies around the world on a broomstick, landing on the roofs of houses and descending down the chimney where she delivers sweets and presents to children who have been good, or coal to those that haven't. They story goes that La Befana was approached by the Three Wise Men who asked her to direct them to the stable where baby Jesus had been born. La Befana was too busy doing the housework and declined. But then she realised she may have made a mistake and gathered up a bag of gifts and set off to search for the baby Jesus. Although she followed the star she was unable to find the stable so she continues to travel the world, searching every house for Jesus. The arrival on 6th

January of La Befana marks the end of the festive holiday season and is celebrated with feasting.

Freya: The first Monday after January 6th was called Old Saxons' Plough Monday, the day when men returned to the plough (or their daily work). The farm labourers would draw a plough from door to door of the parish and solicit plough money. The queen of their celebration was Bessie, a caricature of Freya. Those dragging the plough would dress as white mummers covered with flowers and ribbons.

7th January

Sekhmet: In Egypt, a day to celebrate the Decrees of Sekhmet that were put forward at the end of the reign of Ra.

11th – 15th January

Carmenta/Camenae: The festival of Carmentalia in honour of Carmenta and the Camenae, Roman nymphs of inspiration and prophecy.

11th January

Roman Day of Juturnalia: Juturna was given sacrifices on this day.

12th January

The Roman Festival of Compitalia: Held to honour the spirits of the crossroads and to mark the end of the winter planting season. Each member of the household would hang a woollen doll in the household shrine and give garlic to the Lares (gods of the household). Neighbours would also share honey cakes.

15th January

Vesta – Roman 'Feast of the Ass': This festival was to mark the event in which Vesta was saved by a donkey.

16th January
Hindu festival of Ganesha.

19th January
Norse festival of Thor.

20th January
St Agnes: Night to dream of your future husband...aided by a nod to the St Agnes before you sleep.

30th January
Amun-in-the-Festival-of-Raising-Heaven: The day of bringing branches of the ished tree (sacred tree of the sun god Iunu) including the ceremony of filling the sacred eye of Iunu in Ancient Egypt.

31st January
Hecate: Make offerings to this moon goddess on the last night of the month, preferably at a crossroads.

January/February
Hindu Celebration of Vasant Panchami: Festival for the birthday of the goddess Saraswati. This is celebrated on the 5th day of the bright fortnight of the lunar month of Magha (which falls during Jan/Feb). This celebration also welcomes the beginning of the spring season.

Mid January
Lord Krishna: The celebration of Lohri falls in mid January, marking the end of the coldest month of the year and a time when Lord Krishna manifests himself.

January Full Moon
Thor: Minor Norse feast honouring Thor, the protector of

Midgard. During this time, the height of the storm season, Thor's power is invoked to drive back the frost giant Jotuns so that spring may return to Midgard.

Meditation

Take a deep breath in through your nose and a long sigh out through your mouth. Feel any tension in your body start to melt away as you become comfortable and relaxed. Take another breath in through your nose, the air going deep into your stomach, then slowly and gently release the breath out through your mouth.

Your everyday thoughts and worries fade away as you bring your attention solely to your breath as it moves gently in and slowly out. The world around you starts to dissipate and as it slips away you open your mind's eye to find yourself in a winter landscape.

All around you is a blanket of white snow for as far as the eye can see. It glitters and gleams like a carpet of crystals as you look out across the landscape. In the distance you see a glimpse of what appears to be smoke and you decide to investigate. You pull your thick coat around you and begin to make your way towards the smoke.

As you walk you hear the gentle crunch of your footsteps in the snow and you see your breath as it hits the cold air. But, other than you, there are no other sounds, it is as if the land is sleeping. You stop for a moment and look back at your footsteps in the snow and you see where your path has led you so far and you look ahead at the fresh fallen snow and wonder where your journey will lead you... A path as yet untrod.

You shiver in the cold and continue on your journey in search of warmth. The land starts to make a gentle incline and as you reach the top you see below you a stone circle with an inviting campfire in the middle. You hurriedly make your way towards the fire as your feet and fingers are feeling the cold now. As you reach the fire you notice a female figure who beckons you to come and sit with her.

You join her by the fire and sit quietly as she shares with you her name. Take time with this goddess and ask any questions you may have.

You sense it is time to leave the warmth of the fire. As you stand up, the goddess gives you a gift as a reminder of your time with her. You leave the stone circle with a feeling of clarity and a new-found direction. As you step out onto the crisp white snow, you feel the meditation starting to slip away as you begin to join the real world again.

You become aware of your breath. Take a deep cleansing breath in and a long sigh out, wiggle your toes, wiggle your fingers and when you are ready open your eyes.

Take as long as you need to come back into the room. Write down any messages you were given on your journey.

Energy/Spell Work

January is not only a month for inner work, but also brings the magical properties to help you with your poetic side (nope I haven't got one either but we can try...) as well as your aspirations, bringing balance to your emotions, to bring clarity and truth and also work with divination to help you see how to plan your year. This is also a good month to work with strengthening your connection to the divine, hopefully bringing some enlightenment with it too. Do spell work for:

- Inner work
- Poetry
- Aspirations
- Balancing your emotions
- Clarity
- Truth
- Divination
- Spiritual connections
- Enlightenment

Moon Lore

Our ancient ancestors tracked the passing of time by the phases of the moon. The full moon marking the start of the month, or moonth, and each lunation lasting approximately 29 days.

Gradually each moon was given a name or a label, as we humans like to do. These names would be dictated by what was happening weather wise, like Snow Moon, Ice Moon or what activities were taking place – Harvest Moon or Hunting Moon, for example. Unfortunately, there is no definitive list of names we can give, but throughout this course we will provide examples and more importantly we invite you to create your own list of names.

The January moon is often named Wolf Moon. Wolves would wait at the edge of villages and howl with hunger during the winter months. We are reminded of this as the winter storms rage and howl, asking us to appreciate the beauty in this fierce side of nature. January also brings with it the start of our calendar year and an energy that is challenging and confusing. Beginnings should be a time of emergence, making plans, setting goals and resolutions. But for anyone who lives in the northern hemisphere it is the height of winter, time for deep withdrawal and hibernation. Try to flow with the energy rather than fight against it. Work to cultivate your inner power and confront your personal truths.

Names for the January Moon Include
Wolf Moon, Quiet Moon, Storm Moon, Chaste Moon, Cold Moon and Ice Moon.

In the Celtic Tree Calendar
Birch Moon: 24th December-20th January; new beginnings, goal setting, creativity and fertility
Rowan Moon: 21st January-17th February; preparation, sowing seeds, astral travel, protection

During this month's full moon go outside if you can and soak up her energies, let her speak to you and see what names come to you.

Ritual

We believe that personal rituals should be...well personal! So we have given you an outline guide for your own ritual, but it is up to you to invoke the deity/deities of your choice. One relevant to this month would be good because that's the idea of this course, but if someone else is shouting 'pick me, pick me' don't ignore them. Add in your own individual ideas and style and make the ritual your own.

- Cast the circle
- Call in the quarters
- Invoke deity
- Smudge
- Work some magic or divination or just sit quietly and meditate
- Feast...
- Thank and dismiss the quarters
- Thank and bid farewell to deity
- Close the circle
- And don't forget to ground!

Crystals

Crystals have often been associated with each month and/or the magical energy that the month brings. Try popping one in your pocket, on your altar or meditate with one this month. Again go with your intuition but here are some to get you started:

- Garnet
- Onyx
- Jet
- Chrysoprase
- Rose quartz
- Pink tourmaline
- Rhodochrosite

- Ruby
- Moss agate
- Amber
- Fire opal
- Clear quartz

Our Favourite Gem for January – Rose Quartz
A stone of the heart, love, peace, romance and relationships, it is also a very good 'all rounder'. Rose quartz is an exceptional healing stone for most issues, especially emotional ones.

Children love this stone and it works well for issues from calming a baby through to easing those teenage tantrums.

A good self esteem stone, it also brings in protection with it. It helps to keep nightmares at bay and bring a peaceful sleep.

Use it to help you ground after any energy work and in spell workings for fertility or love.

Crystal Grid
You could use the energies of this month to make a crystal grid. Start with a crystal in the centre and add your intent, if it is for business success you could put a business card under the centre crystal then add crystals going around in a spiral or a mandala pattern fanning out from the centre. I like to add herbs and oracle or tarot cards to my crystal grids too. Once your intuition has told you what crystals to use and where to put them, visualise all the crystals, herbs and cards linking up with a 'web' of white light to bring your intent to reality.

Oil/Incense Blends
Create an essential oil or a loose incense blend to use when you are meditating or just to help you work with the energies of this month. Here are some herbs and scents for incense that we associated with this month, but go with your own ideas:

- Birch
- Marjoram/oregano
- Pine cone
- Crocus
- Snowdrop
- Rosemary
- Chickweed
- Ash
- Rowan
- Bay
- Chervil
- Parsley
- Sage
- Thyme
- Nuts
- Musk
- Mimosa
- Grapefruit
- Lemon
- Orange
- Lavender
- Mint
- Juniper
- Cedarwood
- Cypress
- Bergamot
- Frankincense

Our Favourite Herb for January – Juniper (Juniperus communes)
This is a herb that is old as the hills, dating back to Neolithic times apparently (personally I don't remember that far back).

Keep a sprig of juniper above the door for protection and to keep negative energy out. It has very strong protective properties that keep out all sorts of evil demons.

If you have had something stolen you can petition the spirit of the juniper bush to bring the article back to you and justice to be served.

Wear juniper berries in an amulet to bring love to you and to keep you healthy, also use it in healing workings.

Use in incense blends to purify and cleanse, bring clarity and also to aid with psychic powers. Juniper has strong connections to the spirit world and the afterlife.

Juniper also works well in moon magic, on the dark of the moon.

Essential Oil Recipes for New Beginnings
This oil will help clear out old negative vibes and bring in a new start.

7 drops grapefruit
3 drops lemon
5 drops orange
4 drops lavender
3 drops juniper
2 drops mint

Silent Earth Oil
If you are still in hibernation mode try this silent earth oil.

3 drops patchouli
2 drops cypress
2 drops vertiver

Altar
We would love for you to create an altar for the month. Go with your heart, but think about what this month means to you, what the weather is like, what the magical energy represents and if a goddess came to you then a representation of her would be

good too.

I like to put representations of snow or snowflakes on my altar in January and something that makes me think of my home and hearth.

Mandala

Mandala is a Sanskrit word meaning circle and is a spiritual and ritual symbol that represents the universe. A mandala will often have a square with four gates containing a circle with a centre point, but there are many variations.

Working with mandalas, whether you draw your own or colour in one that has already been created, can be a very relaxing and a surprisingly meditative exercise. You can find lots of free mandalas to download on the internet and colour, but also have a go at creating your own mandala for this month or for a particular goddess.

Pop on some quiet music, get your crayons out, release your inner child and allow yourself to be drawn into the mandala creation...you might be surprised what inspirations you find...

Once your mandala is finished, pop it on your altar.

Spirit Doll

Spirit dolls, poppets, goddess dolls...lots of different names from different cultures, but we thought it would be interesting to create a spirit doll, poppet or goddess representation for each month. Use whatever materials you have to hand or find easiest to work with – felt, cloth, string, Fimo, modelling clay...get creative.

Channel the energy of this month into your creation or add the characteristics and symbols of your chosen goddess.

If you make a doll from felt or material you can add herbs, spices and crystals to the inside too. If you work with clay or Fimo you can also incorporate herbs and crystals into the design.

The finished dolls will carry your very own magical energy

with them together with the spirit of the month or the goddess you intended. Keep them on your altar.

Goddess Beauty

If you're like us then you have probably over indulged during the holiday season. So what better way to help you detox than with a lovely relaxing bath? This recipe will help release toxins and soothe away any residual stress.

Lavender Detox Bath

1 cup (200g) Epsom salts
1 cup (128g) baking soda
10 drops lavender essential oil

Pour all the ingredients into hot bath water, then soak in the bath for 20 minutes. Make sure you cover your entire body, up to your chin if possible.

Once you get out of the bath make sure you drink plenty of water as you will have lost fluids due to perspiring.

Goddess Gift

The divine provides us with gifts...and we encourage you to step outside and see what the goddess, the divine, Mother Nature, has gifted you with.

It might be a feather, a pebble, a shell or maybe a leaf from a tree. Whatever you are gifted with you can add to your altar or maybe, if you are feeling artistic, you could create something with it.

A twig becomes a wand, a shell becomes a pendant, a feather becomes a smudge fan...think outside the box.

Medicine Bag

We have goddess medicine bags that we work with, just a square of material tied with a piece of thong, but inside we have representations of each goddess we have worked with. It helps us to keep a record of our journey, but also provides a focus for meditation and spiritual workings.

If you would like to create your own you can use a square of fabric. A bag made from felt or fabric works well too.

Each time you work with a different goddess ask them what symbol you should use to represent them in your medicine bag...you may be surprised.

By the end of this course you will have a wonderful collection of spiritual goddess items to keep in your own medicine bag.

Meditation Beads

Your mind can sometimes tend to wander when you are meditating, which leads to a loss of concentration. For practising meditation, meditation beads can act as a kind of 'anchor', or grounding point, enabling you to focus better. This can be extremely useful, especially if you are feeling tired when you meditate.

Conversely, if your mind is too active and over-energised, meditation beads will prevent you from becoming distracted or daydreaming. And, because the beads are moved in rhythm with your breathing, it helps you maintain your concentration.

At the end of this course you should have your own set of personal deities so you could create a string of meditation beads using one bead for each of your deities. It could be in the form of a necklace containing a bead for each of your twelve goddesses or you could make individual bracelets or pendants, one for each month.

The beads don't need to be used solely for meditation, you can use them throughout the day. When you awake, hold the beads and run them through your fingers and connect with their energy. This will set you up with positive intentions for the day.

Carry the beads with you in your pocket or bag, take them out during the day to remind you to stay grounded and focus on your tasks. Trust me, I need these all the time for focusing!

Hold the beads when you feel stressed or spacey to help bring you back centred and calm.

Finish your day the way you started by running the beads through your fingers and count your blessings. Release the negative points from your day and allow them to be replaced by the positive. Feel the good energy from the fabulous points of your day wash over you.

You also don't need to spend huge amounts of money. There are some beautiful meditation beads out there (often called prayer beads or malas), but you can make them yourself with whatever beads you have. There is no need to create a set of beads using expensive natural stones (although they are beautiful and full of natural energy). If all you have are wooden or plastic beads then use them, raid your children's play box even! The idea of the beads is to use them as a focus, so even if you have a string of dried peas the intention is the same.

Feasting

We have included a recipe for each month – basically we don't need any excuse to include a cake recipe...but if you feel inclined to pop into the kitchen to bake we have given monthly suggestions on cakes to use in ritual to honour the goddess or just because they are yummy. If you love to cook you don't have to stop at cake, you could create a meal in honour of the goddess you are working with for the month (or just order a takeaway).

Orange Polenta Cake

For the cake
200g (7oz) unsalted butter
200g (7oz) soft brown sugar
200g (7oz) ground almonds

100g (3½oz) polenta
3 large eggs
Zest of 2 oranges
1 teaspoon vanilla essence
1 teaspoon orange blossom water
1 teaspoon baking powder
Plain yoghurt to serve

For the syrup
250ml (9fl oz) orange juice
30ml (1fl oz) orange blossom water
5 cardamom pods, crushed
125g caster sugar

Preheat the oven to 160C and grease and line a 20cm springform cake tin.

Beat together the sugar and butter until light and creamy. Beat in the eggs one at a time and then add the vanilla essence.

In a bowl, combine the ground almonds, polenta, orange zest, orange blossom water and baking powder. Then stir that into the sugar and butter. Pour the mixture into the cake tin and bake for 40-50 minutes. The top should be a light brown and the cake will come away slightly around the sides of the tin. Leave to cool for 10 minutes before turning out on to a plate. The cake is quite fragile so be gentle.

Then make the syrup by putting all the syrup ingredients into a pan and simmer gently over a low-medium heat until it reduces and slightly thickens. This should take about 10 minutes. Then set it aside to cool.

Prick the cake all over with a skewer and brush gently with the syrup.

Serve with a nice dollop of natural yoghurt and a drizzle of the syrup.

February

February always feels like the start of the turning point. Although it is not spring yet, February sees the beginnings of new growth and even (hopefully) a few sunnier days. And, of course, the beginning of February brings the festival of Imbolc, which is traditionally sacred to the goddess Brighid. This is the month when we celebrate the maiden awaiting the return of her sun god; it is a time for renewal, new beginnings and a good ol' clear out, spring clean, sort clutter and smudge, smudge, smudge...

It is also the time of year for all the baby sheepses to be bouncing around the fields and to celebrate that spring is on its way. Prepare for growth and renewal of all kinds and keep an eye out for the first spring flowers.

Deities

In this part of the course we suggest nine goddesses we associate with this month. Have a read through the information and see if any of them resonate with you. It may be that one of them comes to you in the meditation, it might be that another deity altogether greets you...go with your intuition. We have also included a list of some deities that have celebrations or feast days within this month too.

Boann

Irish goddess associated with flowing waters and rivers, spiritual insight and poetry. She brings inspiration and clarity to the mind while opening the soul to the divine.

Chang-O

Chang-O is a Chinese goddess of the moon. Along with her husband, Chang-O was banished from the heavens to live on earth as a mortal. She was so desperate to return to her former place of glory that she took an immortality pill, not just one dose, but also her husband's allocation too. She floated up to the moon, but was then destined to spend the rest of eternity on her lonesome. During a festival in China in her honour women pray to her to send their soul mate to them. She is also given offerings of sweet foods and incense.

Parvati

Parvati is a Hindu goddess of all things feminine and she represents womanhood in all its glory. She is part of the triple goddess triad with Durga and Kali Ma, Parvati representing the maiden aspect. With her skill and patience she seduced the god Shiva and manipulated him with her womanly wiles to tell her all the secrets of the universe. She is the patroness of dancers, poets and artists. Her name translated means 'she who is of the mountains'.

Venus

Roman goddess of beauty and sexual love, and in many important respects similar to the Hellenic Aphrodite. She had considerable authority and influence in agrarian concerns, in her case gardens and flowering plants. She is the morning and the evening star, and the daughter of the sea. She dispels troubles and turmoil, giving out happiness and joy. She is the patron to prostitutes and heals sexual issues.

Shakti

Shakti is the divine force, manifesting to destroy demonic forces and restore balance. Every god in Hinduism has his Shakti and without that energy they have no power. So Shakti is the mother goddess, the source of all, the universal principle of energy, power or creativity. The worship of Shakti as this energy is the main objective of tantra yoga. Shakti is inseparable from the one who beholds her, the Shakti-man, the masculine principle or universal father. Shakti-man is called Brahma or Shiva. The play of female energy has no beginning and no end. Although it is restless, the energy moves through alternating periods of motion and rest, during which order is re-established. Tantra believes that as long as the phenomenal world exists, it is the universal mother who is the creator, preserver.

Bast

A goddess of occultism and magic, she is the female aspect of the sun god Ra. In earlier images she is portrayed as having the head of a lioness; later these images show her with the head of a cat. Egyptian goddess of sensual pleasure, protector of the household, bringer of health, and the guardian saint of fire fighters – she was the original mistress of multi-tasking. Also called Bastet or Basthet, the goddess Bast is widely known today as the 'cat goddess'. Legend has it that, by day, Bast would ride through the sky with her father, the sun god Ra, in his boat pulling the sun through the sky.

Selene

Selene (derived from a root meaning 'light' or 'gleam') is the Greek goddess of the moon, the lunar disc. Selene is the Titan goddess of the moon, and rules lunar magic and sensuality. She aids sleep and dream prophecy.

The Muses

The Muses are made up from nine Greek goddesses who represent music, song and dance along with knowledge and inspiration. They were the daughters of Zeus and Mnemosyne (the personification of memory) and they were also considered water nymphs.

Hebe

Greek goddess of youth and the cupbearer to the gods, she

served ambrosia at the feasts. She is also the patron goddess of young brides and an attendant to Aphrodite.

Feast/Celebration Days
We have listed here the feast and celebration days for deities (we have included gods as well as goddesses) throughout February from various cultures and pantheons. These are taken from our own research...we apologise for any errors, but history is a fickle thing and calendars have changed over the years.

1st February

Demeter/ Persephone: Celebrating the return of Persephone to her mother Demeter after her descent into the Otherworld.

Brighid/Brigantia: Celebrating St Brighid's Day, the festival of Imbolc and also the Christian celebration of Candlemas (sometimes celebrated on February 2nd) all with the theme of recognising and welcoming the first day of spring, new beginnings and new initiations.

Ptah: Egyptian festival of Ptah; day of return of the image of the deity in the festival 'Amun-in-the-festival-of-raising-heaven'.

2nd February

Februa: An old Roman custom of burning candles to the goddess Februa, mother of Mars, to scare away evil spirits.

The Virgin Mary: Christian day of the Holy Virgin Mary when candles are lit.

Disting: Norse festival of the Idises, when the effects of winter are beginning to lessen and the world prepares itself for spring. Disting is characterised by preparing the land for planting. In ancient times, Disting was the time when the cattle were counted and one's wealth was tallied; thus making it a festival of prosperity as well. It was said that new calves born during Disting were a sign of great abundance for the coming year.

11ᵗʰ-13ᵗʰ February

Anthesteria: Held annually for three days (11th-13th) in the month of Anthesterion (February-March). Although its name indicates a festival of flowers (anthos), the festival focused primarily on opening the new wine and on placating the spirits of the dead. On the evening of the first day, called Pithoigia (jar-opening), casks of the previous vintage were taken to the sanctuary of Dionysus in the Marshes and libations were offered to the god of wine and sampled by the entire household. The rooms and the drinking vessels were adorned with spring flowers, as were the children over three years of age. The second day, named Choes (pitchers), was a time of merrymaking. The people dressed themselves gaily, some in the disguise of the mythical personages in the suite of Dionysus, and paid a round of visits to their acquaintances. The primary activity of the day was a drinking competition, in which participants sat at separate tables and competed in silence at draining a chous (a five-litre container) of wine. Slaves had a share as well. Miniature choes were given to children as toys, and 'First Choes' was a rite of passage.

14ᵗʰ February

St Valentine: A descendant of Lupercalia perhaps, in the middle of February names of willing young ladies were put in a box and shaken up. Each young suitor would draw out one at random. The girl thus won to remain his companion while the festivities lasted.

Valisblot: Many modern Asatruar celebrate Valisblot, or Vali's Feast, even though there is no historical precedent for associating Odin's youngest son with this festival, other than the name Vali associated with 'Valentine'. The hero Svenfjotli, son of Sigimund, was reputed to have been born at this time, and often blots are drunk to him as well.

15ᵗʰ February

Lupa, the She Wolf/Faunus/Inuus: Lupercalia was celebrated to worship the she-wolf who suckled Romulus and Remus, legendary founders of Rome. It started with a group of specially appointed priests gathering at the Lupercal, a cave at the bottom of the Palatine Hill. The priests would offer a sacrifice of a goat, and anoint the Lupercii (young male participants) on their foreheads with the blood. The blood was wiped away with milk by other priests, and the young men laughed at them. The Lupercii then skinned the sacrificed goat and ripped the hide into strips, which they tied around their naked waists. They then got drunk, and ran around Rome striking everyone they met with goatskin thongs. Young women who were touched in this manner were thought to be specially blessed, especially in regards to fertility and procreation.

Lupercalia was a very ancient festival, and may have originally been a festival for purification and fertility in honour of either Faunus or Inuus.

21ˢᵗ February

Anunitu: The heavenly one was a Babylonian goddess with one fish between her legs and one across her breasts. This was a day of celebration in her honour.

The Feralia: The closing festival of the Parentalia. During the Feralia, Roman families would picnic at the tombs of their deceased family members and give libations to the dearly departed. It was believed that the shades of the dead could walk upon the earth above their graves during Feralia.

February 22ⁿᵈ

Caristia: Also known as the Cara Cognatio, this was held to honour the Roman goddess of agreement, Concordia. During this festival, family members would gather in the home and feast together and then make offerings to the household deities and settle arguments.

23rd February

Birthday of the Chinese God of Wealth: A time to make money trees for prosperity.

Diasia: Great festival celebrated in Athens in honour of Zeus. The whole town took part, the wealthier citizens offered victims while the poorer classes burned incense accompanied by plenty of feasting and a fair.

26th February

Mut: A powerful, protective and primordial vulture goddess of Egypt, later in her lioness form also the wife of the god Amun of Karnak and mother of the moon god Khonsu. Every High Priestess Queen of Egypt wore the vulture goddess Mut as a head-dress to signify their spiritual development, opening of the third eye and blending of her head with the goddess of life and death herself.

27th February

Equirria: This festival involved racing horses to honour the Roman god Mars. It was held in the Campus Martius or the Campus Martialis on the Caelian Hill if the Campus Martius was flooded. The Equirria was said to have been founded by Romulus.

5th-17th February

The Fornacalia: Held in honour of bread, and the ovens used to dry grains. This Roman festival was movable, and could have been held any time between February 5th and February 17th.

17th February

The Quirinalia: Roman festival of Quirinus, it signalled the end of the Fornacalia. It was also known as the 'Feast of Fools'.

13th-21st February

Parentalia: This festival honoured the Di Manes. It began at dawn on February 13th with private ceremonies and ended with the public Feralia on February 21st. During the Parentalia every temple was closed, marriages were forbidden to take place, magistrates were not allowed to wear anything signifying their office, and all Romans were expected to give offerings to the deceased at the necropolis located outside the city walls.

23rd February

Terminalia: On this day, landowners would honour the boundaries of their land at the boundary markers and honour the god Terminus. Rome's public boundary stone in the temple of Jupiter Optimus Maximus was also honoured. Garlands were placed over the boundary stones and altars were built near them. Offerings of grain and honey were given by the children, and the adults would offer wine and pig blood. Everyone was dressed in white and was required to keep silent throughout the offerings. A picnic feast was held at the end of the ritual.

Amburbium: This ritual was held in Rome to clean and purify the city and everything in it. The actual date changed from year to year, though it was usually held after the ides.

Thaipusam: Thaipusam is an important festival observed by the Hindus of southern India during the Tamil month of Thai (January-February). Outside India, it is celebrated mainly by the Tamil-speaking community settled in Malaysia, Singapore, South Africa, Sri Lanka and elsewhere around the world.

Thaipusam is dedicated to the Hindu god Murugan, the son of Shiva and Parvati. Murugan is also known as Kartikeya, Subramaniam, Sanmukha, Shadanana, Skanda and Guha. It is believed that on this day, goddess Parvati presented a lance to Lord Murgan to vanquish the demon army of Tarakasura and combat their evil deeds. Therefore, Thaipusam is a celebration of the victory of good over evil.

Maha Shivratri: The night of the worship of Lord Shiva occurs on the 14th night of the new moon during the dark half of the month of Phalguna. It falls on a moonless February night, when Hindus offer special prayer to the lord of destruction. Shivratri (Sanskrit 'ratri' means 'night') is the night when he is said to have performed the Tandava Nritya, or the dance of primordial creation, preservation and destruction. The festival is observed for one day and one night only.

Meditation

Take a deep breath in through your nose and a long sigh out through your mouth. Feel any tension in your body start to melt away as you become comfortable and relaxed. Take another breath in through your nose, the air going deep into your stomach, then slowly and gently release the breath out through your mouth.

Your everyday thoughts and worries fade away as you bring your attention solely to your breath as it moves gently in and slowly out. The world around you starts to dissipate and as it slips away you open your mind's eye to find yourself on a country lane.

It is almost dawn on a cold morning that is still in the clutches of winter. The sky has that strange grey, expectant hue that comes just before the sunrise. As you walk down the lane the sun comes up over the horizon, seeming to climb a little higher with each step you take. The faster you walk the quicker the sun starts to climb until beautiful winter sunshine reveals more of the world around you.

You notice that the snow has started to melt and you can see the odd blade of grass poking through the now very thin blanket of white. The trees are still bare, but now have teams of snowdrops surrounding their base, like little cheerleaders encouraging the new buds.

Caught up in the wonder of the first signs of the earth awakening you didn't realise that you had reached the end of the lane and are now standing at a five-bar gate. You push open the gate and carefully close it behind you. The little lane has led you into a large field with barns and buildings on the left hand side. You hear sounds coming from the big barn and so you make your way towards it.

As you approach you realise the sounds are the gentle bleating of sheep that are lambing. You enter the barn that is only a little warmer than it is outside. There are sheep and lambs in little pens within the barn. Some lambs are being washed my the new mothers, some are feeding on the nutritious ewe's milk, standing on shaking, wobbly legs, and others are still in the process of being born into the world. You watch for a little while in awe of the miracle of life happening right before your eyes

'Would you like to help me my child?' A woman's voice brings you back from your thoughts. She hands you a newborn lamb and a bottle of milk. 'Her mother didn't make the birth but this one is a fighter,' she says.

You feel overwhelmed with sadness for the lamb, but at the same time you must be as strong as she is.

And so you fight back the tears and you feed the lamb from the bottle. As you watch the hungry little girl feed, the woman tells you her name and shares a message that is just for you...

The lamb has now finished the bottle and starts to fall asleep in your arms, and so you hand her back to what you now know is a goddess of February. Before you leave the barn, the goddess gives you a gift as a reminder of the message she shared.

You open the barn door and step back outside. You feel the meditation starting to slip away as you begin to join the real world again.

You become aware of your breath. Take a deep cleansing breath in and a long sigh out, wiggle your toes, wiggle your fingers and, when you are ready, open your eyes.

Take as long as you need to come back into the room. Write down any messages you were given on your journey.

Energy/Spell Work

Of course with Valentine's Day slap bang in the middle of February, it is a good month to work some love magic. It is also a good month to work magic for:

- Dedications
- Initiations
- Astral travel work
- Personal power
- Problem solving
- Friendship issues
- Success
- Personal protection
- Love
- Divination
- Aspirations
- Balance of emotions
- Clarity
- Truth
- Spiritual connections

Moon Lore

Our ancient ancestors tracked the passing of time by the phases of the moon. The full moon marking the start of the month, or moonth, and each lunation lasting approximately 29 days. Gradually each moon was given a name or a label, as we humans like to do. These names would be dictated by what was happening weather wise, like Snow Moon, Ice Moon or what activities were taking place – Harvest Moon or Hunting Moon, for example. Unfortunately, there is no definitive list of names we can give, but throughout this course we will provide examples and more importantly we invite you to create your own list of names.

Storms can be their most violent just before they end, just as

February can bring a fierce and brutal end to winter. The world may seem to be wrapped up in the winter's sleep, but just under the surface new life is waiting for the storm to die down before it to pushes through.

Names for the February Moon Include
Storm Moon, Ice Moon, Snow Moon, Quickening Moon

In the Celtic Tree Calendar
Rowan Moon: 21st January-17th February; preparation, sowing the seeds, astral travel, protection
Ash Moon: 18th February-17th March; travel, transformation, spiritual journeys.

During this month's full moon go outside if you can and soak up her energies, let her speak to you and see what names come to you.

Ritual
We believe that personal rituals should be...well personal! So we have given you an outline guide for your own ritual, but it is up to you to invoke the deity/deities of your choice, relevant to this month would be good because that's the idea of this course, but if someone else is shouting 'pick me, pick me' don't ignore them. Add in your own individual ideas and style and make the ritual your own.

- Cast the circle
- Call in the quarters
- Invoke deity
- Smudge
- Work some magic or divination or just sit quietly and meditate
- Feast...

- Thank and dismiss the quarters
- Thank and bid farewell to deity
- Close the circle
- And don't forget to ground!

Crystals

Crystals have often been associated with each month and/or the magical energy that the month brings. Try popping one in your pocket, on your altar or meditate with one this month. Again go with your intuition but here are some to get you started:

- Amethyst
- Ammolite
- Angelite
- Garnet
- Jasper
- Imperial topaz
- Onyx
- Aquamarine
- Fluorite
- Turquoise
- Ruby
- Bloodstone

Our Favourite Gem for February – Turquoise
If you need help with your throat chakra or communication then this is the stone for the job. It can also help to diffuse arguments and to help you say what you really mean.

It is a good detox stone for the whole body and system (don't eat it obviously…).

Turquoise is a stone of prosperity and success, but also for protection.

Give a piece of turquoise to a child to carry if they are being bullied or to give courage and boost self-esteem for shy children.

Turquoise not only absorbs negative energy, but also brings wisdom and helps boost your psychic abilities.

It brings energy and balance and helps sort out any emotional issues.

Crystal Grid
You could use the energies of this month to make a crystal grid. Start with a crystal in the centre and add your intent, if it is for business success you could put a business card under the centre crystal then add crystals going around in a spiral or a mandala pattern fanning out from the centre. I like to add herbs and oracle or tarot cards to my crystal grids too. Once your intuition has told you what crystals to use and where to put them, visualise all the crystals, herbs and cards linking up with a 'web' of white light to bring your intent to reality.

Oil/Incense Blends
Create an essential oil or a loose incense blend to use when you are meditating or just to help you work with the energies of this month. Here are some herbs and scents for incense that we associated with this month, but go with your own ideas:

- Cypress
- Cinnamon
- Lavender
- Patchouli
- Lemon
- Orange
- Sandalwood
- Rose
- Ginger
- Clove
- Myrrh
- Frankincense

- Ylang Ylang
- Palma rosa
- Bay
- Mint
- Rosemary
- Thyme
- Oregano
- Sage
- Basil

Our Favourite Herb for February – Nettles (Urtica dioica)
Hans Christian Anderson wrote about stinging nettles in his story The Wild Swans, the princess having to weave coats for them out of nettles.

Nettles are also said to mark the place where elves live. Carry nettles with you not only to protect against lightning, but also to draw money to you.

Historically nettles have held the power of protection quite often against demons and witches...eep! They have also been used as anaesthetic and also as a weird kind of rheumatism remedy (apparently the pain of the sting puts the rheumatism pain to shame).

The leaves of the nettle also make a very good green dye.

Nettle can be used to remove curses and send back hexes; it also works well for exorcism and to protect against negative energies and avert danger.

Use in amulets and medicine bags to allay fear and ward against ghosts.

Nettles are very good for putting into poppets or witches bottles to remove curses. Make a magic powder with dried nettles and sprinkle around your property to keep out negative energies. Use nettles in medicine pouches for healing.

Essential Oil/Incense Recipe – Maiden Awakening Oil
Mix together:

   3 drops frankincense
   2 drops lavender
   2 drops orange

Altar

We would love for you to create an altar for the month. Go with your heart, but think about what this month means to you, what the weather is like, what the magical energy represents. If a goddess came to you then a representation of her would be good too.

Perhaps make it look spring-like with spring flowers, Brighid's crosses, seeds, fire symbols, wands and of course lots of candles.

Mandala

Mandala is a Sanskrit word meaning circle and is a spiritual and ritual symbol that represents the universe. A mandala will often have a square with four gates containing a circle with a centre point, but there are many variations.

Working with mandalas, whether you draw your own or colour in one that has already been created, can be a very relaxing and a surprisingly meditative exercise. You can find lots of free mandalas to download on the internet and colour, but also have a go at creating your own mandala for this month or for a particular goddess.

Pop on some quiet music, get your crayons out, release your inner child and allow yourself to be drawn into the mandala creation...you might be surprised what inspirations you find...

Once your mandala is finished, pop it on your altar.

Spirit Doll

Spirit dolls, poppets, goddess dolls...lots of different names from different cultures, but we thought it would be interesting to create a spirit doll, poppet or goddess representation for each month. Use whatever materials you have to hand or find easiest to work with – felt, cloth, string, Fimo, modelling clay...get creative.

Channel the energy of this month into your creation or add the characteristics and symbols of your chosen goddess.

If you make a doll from felt or material you can add herbs, spices and crystals to the inside too. If you work with clay or Fimo you can also incorporate herbs and crystals into the design.

The finished dolls will carry your very own magical energy with them together with the spirit of the month or the goddess you intended. Keep them on your altar.

Goddess Beauty

Hair can get very dry in the winter months so treat yourself to this nourishing hair conditioner.

1 can of coconut milk
1 ripe avocado
2 tablespoons of pure honey
2 tablespoons of olive or avocado oil

Add all the ingredients into a blender and mix on high speed. You should be left with what looks like a smoothie.

Apply the mixture evenly through your hair. Depending on length and thickness you may need to split your hair into sections to make sure you cover it all.

Once covered, put your hair into a bun or ponytail and leave for 15 -30 minutes. Then rinse and style as normal.

Goddess Gift

The divine provides us with gifts...and we encourage you to step outside and see what the goddess, the divine, Mother Nature, has gifted you with.

It might be a feather, a pebble, a shell or maybe a leaf from a tree. Whatever you are gifted with you can add to your altar or maybe, if you are feeling artistic, you could create something with it.

A twig becomes a wand, a shell becomes a pendant, a feather becomes a smudge fan...think outside the box.

Medicine Bag

We have goddess medicine bags that we work with, just a square of material tied with a piece of thong, but inside we have representations of each goddess we have worked with. It helps us to keep a record of our journey, but also provides a focus for meditation and spiritual workings.

If you would like to create your own you can use a square of fabric. A bag made from felt or fabric works well too.

Each time you work with a different goddess ask them what symbol you should use to represent them in your medicine bag...you may be surprised.

By the end of this course you will have a wonderful collection of spiritual goddess items to keep in your own medicine bag.

Meditation Beads

Your mind can sometimes tend to wander when you are meditating, which leads to a loss of concentration. For practising meditation, meditation beads can act as a kind of 'anchor', or grounding point, enabling you to focus better. This can be extremely useful, especially if you are feeling tired when you meditate.

Conversely, if your mind is too active and over-energised, meditation beads will prevent you from becoming distracted or daydreaming. And, because the beads are moved in rhythm with your breathing, it helps you maintain your concentration.

At the end of this course you should have your own set of personal deities so you could create a string of meditation beads using one bead for each of your deities. It could be in the form of a necklace containing a bead for each of your twelve goddesses or you could make individual bracelets or pendants, one for each month.

The beads don't need to be used solely for meditation, you can use them throughout the day. When you awake, hold the beads and run them through your fingers and connect with their energy. This will set you up with positive intentions for the day.

Carry the beads with you in your pocket or bag, take them out during the day to remind you to stay grounded and focus on your tasks. Trust me, I need these all the time for focusing!

Hold the beads when you feel stressed or spacey to help bring you back centred and calm.

Finish your day the way you started by running the beads through your fingers and count your blessings. Release the negative points from your day and allow them to be replaced by the positive. Feel the good energy from the fabulous points of your day wash over you.

You also don't need to spend huge amounts of money. There are some beautiful meditation beads out there (often called prayer beads or malas), but you can make them yourself with whatever beads you have. There is no need to create a set of beads using expensive natural stones (although they are beautiful and full of natural energy). If all you have are wooden or plastic beads then use them, raid your children's play box even! The idea of the beads is to use them as a focus so even if you have a string of dried peas the intention is the same.

Feasting
We have included a recipe for each month – basically we don't

need any excuse to include a cake recipe...but if you feel inclined to pop into the kitchen to bake we have given monthly suggestions on cakes to use in ritual to honour the goddess or just because they are yummy. If you love to cook you don't have to stop at cake, you could create a meal in honour of the goddess you are working with for the month (or just order a takeaway).

Maple Syrup Cake

225g (8oz) butter, softened
225g (8oz) light muscovado sugar
4 large eggs
100ml (3½fl oz) maple syrup
350g (12oz) self raising flour
2 level teaspoons baking powder
½ teaspoon ground ginger

Preheat the oven to 160C/Gas 3. Lightly grease a deep 8 inch cake tin and line the base with baking parchment.

Put all the ingredients into a bowl and mix well until evenly blended. Spoon the mixture into the cake tin and level the surface.

Bake for 1-1½ hours until well risen, golden and springy to the touch. Allow it to cool slightly then turn the cake out onto a wire rack and leave to cool completely.

I like to serve this as it is, but you could mix some icing sugar with water and drizzle it over the top to create icing or serve the cake warm with custard.

March

The month of March can be freezing cold and in some places still knee deep in snow, but as the month progresses it starts to bring with it the promise of brighter, warmer days.

March heralds the arrival of spring and the celebration of Ostara, the spring equinox and we hope it also heralds the end to the persistent rain we are likely to have been having. Dark and light are equal on the equinox so it always represents a time of finding balance for me.

And, of course, with Ostara being in March we get to celebrate new life and new beginnings in the form of chocolate eggs and bunnies...who could argue with that? Mother Earth is awakening and feeling the first joys of spring, join in the celebrations and revel in the new and exciting energy. It is a time to plant new seeds, not just in the garden but within your life as well, a time to bring in the inspiration and make wonderful plans for new schemes and adventures.

I know you don't really want to hear this but...think 'spring cleaning' too, not just the house but a whole magical spring clean that includes clearing out old habits and past worries too.

This is the time of the maiden; young, excitable and literally full of the joys of spring.

Deities

In this part of the course we suggest nine goddesses that we associate with this month, have a read through the information and see if any of them resonate with you. It may be that one of them comes to you in the meditation, it might be that another deity altogether greets you...go with your intuition. We have also included a list of some deities that have celebrations or feast days within this month too.

Cybele
This Roman goddess is the mother of gods, fertility and a nature goddess who also protects her people. Her spring festivals were filled with dancing, music, alcohol and orgies. Her main followers were men who had been castrated and dressed as women...who are we to judge?

Iris
A goddess of the rainbow from Greece, she is a messenger of the gods with power over the sky and the sea; she is the bridge between the heavens and earth. A young woman with wings, she is often seen standing beside Hera or Zeus.

Maia
A solitary Greek goddess of spring, she lives in a cave and works with the magic of spring, fertility of the land and midwifery.

Indunn
A youthful Norse goddess, she rules immortality and eternal youth. She is also the keeper of magical apples that bring the spirit of youth. A maiden, she supplies the gods with everlasting life as well as sending strength to those who are weak or sick and she is a patroness of spring.

Eostre
Said to be a Saxon/Germanic goddess of spring, she is a goddess of fertility and is often depicted with painted eggs and surrounded by hares.

Britomartis
Goddess of the mountains, seas and hunting from Crete, she is a chaste virgin goddess who avoids male advances, but sends blessings to the hunters and fishermen. She crosses over from Minoan culture into Greek.

Verbeia

She is an ancient British goddess associated with the river Wharfe depicted holding two snakes and said to manifest into a white horse. She is known to be wild and dangerous, but also has a nurturing and life-giving nature as well.

Butterfly Maiden

The Butterfly Maiden is a Hopi kachina that governs the spring and the fertility of the earth. Kachinas are supernatural beings that control nature and have the spirits of living things such as animals and plants within them. She governs rebirth, beauty, fertility, balance, freedom and nature.

Eos

A Titan goddess from Greece, she is goddess of the dawn and married to Astraeus, the god of dusk. Together they had children that represent the twilight.

Feast/Celebration Days

We have listed here the feast and celebration days for deities (we have included gods as well as goddesses) throughout March from various cultures and pantheons. These are taken from our own research...we apologise for any errors, but history is a fickle thing and calendars have changed over the years...

1st March

The Matronalia: A festival celebrated by Roman matrons, the anniversary of the foundation of the temple of Juno Lucina on the Esquiline. In the houses, prayers were offered for a prosperous wedlock, the women received presents from the men and waited on the slaves. In the temple of the goddess, women and girls prayed to her and brought pious offerings.

Vesta: On every 1st March the Vestal fire was rekindled only by a burning glass or the method of friction by boring a piece of wood from a fruit tree. The withered laurel was withdrawn from the Vestal hearth so that Vesta might show herself dressed in fresh leaves.

5th March
Isis: The Egyptian festival of the ship of Isis was held in recognition of her being patroness of navigation and inventor of the sail.

7th March
Junonalia: In Rome, this day honoured Juno with a procession of 27 girls accompanying a statue of Juno carved out of a cypress tree.

15th March
Kybele: A week-long purification for the Rites of Kybele (Phrygian mother of the gods) began on 22nd March, initiated by a process of reed bearers.

15th March
Anna Parenna: The festival for Anna Parenna, 'goddess of the returning year', was held each year on the first day of the ancient year. Traditionally, Romans would cross the Tiber and 'go abroad' into Etruria and have picnics in flimsy tents or huts made of branches. Both men and women would drink as much alcohol as they could, as it was thought that one would live for as many years as cups of alcohol one could drink on this day. Once finished with the picnic and drinking, the Romans would wander back to their homes in Rome.

Guild Festival: Guilds whose members practised the arts of Minerva had a festival on this day. This was mainly a Plebeian festival, and was celebrated at Minerva's temple in Rome. Weapons used for war were purified during this festival.

16ᵗʰ March

Mounykhion: In honour of Artemis the Greek moon goddess and lady of the beasts. This was started with a procession of people carrying small round cakes called amphiphontes in which small torches were stuck. These were offered to Artemis. Some say the cake was called amphiphon, which can mean 'shining by double light' as they were offered when the sun and the moon were both visible. In ancient times a she-goat was sacrificed.

16ᵗʰ-17ᵗʰ March

Festival of Bacchus: This Roman festival was held to honour the Bacchus in order to convince the god to give a good grape harvest later that year. It was originally a Greek festival held to honour Dionysus.

17ᵗʰ March

Liberalia: A fertility festival celebrated in rural areas, held in honour of Liber Pater and Libera. Most towns created a large phallus and carted it through the countryside and into the town centre where it stayed until the beginning of the next month. The phallus was decorated by a virtuous woman with flowers, which ensured a good crop at the next harvest. Masks were also hung on fences and crude songs were sung during the procession.

19ᵗʰ -23ʳᵈ March

Minerva: The Greater Quinquatrus was a festival for Minerva as a goddess of the arts. The first day of the festival was dedicated to the arts and those who practised them would give Minerva sacrifices at her temple on the Aventine in Rome.

21ˢᵗ March

Spring Equinox/Ostara: Ostara is a festival of fertility and growth that occurs on the spring equinox, the first day of spring.

On this day, darkness and light are in balance. Ostara is a celebration of renewal and rebirth of nature and warming of the earth.

Artemis: Artemis' favourite animal was believed, all over Greece, to be the hind. From this sacred animal the Athenians called the month (March-April) Artemision. The term became common throughout Greece.

Elaphebolion: Greeks held her festival as goddess of game and hunting at which cakes in the shape of deer were offered up.

Tiamat: The Babylonians celebrated the spring equinox during which the Epic of the Creation of the World was recited twice and probably a series of rituals carried out.

22nd March

Kybele: After a week of fasting and purification the festival properly began.

Astarte/Aphrodite/Venus: The Gardens of Adonis (the dying or dead lover of Astarte/Aphrodite/Venus) were baskets or pots filled with earth in which wheat, barley, lettuce, fennel and flowers were sown and tended for eight days (usually by women).

23rd March

Mars/Nerine: On 23rd March there was a festival of Mars and Nevine, the Sabine goddess who was identified with Athena/Minerva or Aphrodite.

25th March

Hilaria – 'Day of Joy': This festival honoured Attis, and was primarily a festival for the followers of his cult. Several smaller festivals connected to the Hilaria were held on the preceding days, such as the Dies Sanguinis ('Day of Blood') on 24th March, and the Day of Mourning on 23rd March.

Renenutet: Harvest offering to the Egyptian deity Renenutet.

27th March

Renenutet: Granary offering to the Egyptian deity Renenutet.

31st March

Mammitu: The goddess of Fate responsible for fixing destinies. This was a time when the king of Mesopotamia would have his fortune read from a chart and be told what destiny awaited him and the kingdom for the year to come.

Bendis: Bendis was a goddess of the moon among the Thracians; she had power over heaven and earth and was also identified with the Greek Artemis, Hecate and Persephone. A public festival was instituted called the Bendideia at which there were torch races and a procession.

Luna: The Italian goddess of the moon had an ancient sanctuary in Rome on the Aventine, in which as goddess of the month she received worship on the last day of March (which was the first month of the old Roman year).

Good Friday: A day to pay honour to Mary Magdalene.

Hecate/Artemis/Selene/Diana: Hot cross buns are always associated with Easter and Good Friday but they were around long before Christianity. Greeks offered to Apollo, Diana, Hecate and the moon cakes with 'horns' called a 'bous', the cross symbolised the four quarters of the moon. Wheaten cakes marked with a cross have been eaten at the spring festival by many cultures dating far back and, indeed, they were eaten wherever Diana was worshipped and her festival occurred at this time.

Astarte/Venus/Adonis: For the rites of Venus Urania (Astarte) and Adonis at Byblos all the people in mourning entered a deep cave where the image of a young man lay on a bed of flowers and herbs. Whole days passed in prayer and lamentations. Adonia were solemn feasts in honour of Venus and in memory of her beloved Adonis. They lasted two days. On the first, images of Venus and Adonis were carried with huge amounts of ceremony. The Egyptian Queen would herself carry an image of Adonis in procession.

The Corn Mother: During the European ritual of the Corn Mother and Corn Daughter the last sheaf of corn, called the Corn Mother, was made up into the shape of a woman by the oldest married woman in the village. The finest ears were plucked out of it and made into a wreath which, twined with flowers, were carried on the head of the prettiest girl in the village. On Easter Eve the grain was rubbed out of it by a seven-year-old girl and scattered among the young corn. The fertilising power of the Corn Mother was brought out by scattering seed taken from her body among the new corn and her influence over animal life was indicated by placing the straw in a manger.

Astarte/Ishtar: A time to honour Astarte, Queen of Heaven, whose name was used by the people of Nineveh and found on Assyrian monuments as Ishtar, and her consort Bel. The egg is a symbol of Astarte at Easter.

Isis/Kybele: The spring festivals of Isis and Kybele took place in Egypt generally in March.

Holi – The Festival of Colours: This is undoubtedly the most fun-filled and boisterous of Hindu festival. It is an occasion that brings in unadulterated joy and mirth, fun and play, music and dance, and, of course, lots of bright colours. It is a festival celebrating the passing of winter and the beginning of spring. Every year it takes place on the day after the full moon in early March and glorifies good harvest and fertility of the land. It is also time for spring harvest. The new crop refills the stores in every household and perhaps such abundance accounts for the riotous merriment during Holi.

Nyepi: Nyepi is New Year's Day in Bali; Nyepi is a day of celebration and of silence – a day to remember not only oneself, but also the state of the universe before creation. Usually Nyepi falls in mid-March. Following the Hindu lunar calendar, Nyepi begins the Saka year in the month of Chaitra (March). In India the Saka calendar begins with purnima or full moon, but in Bali it starts with amavasya or moonless night. Nyepi begins with fasting and silence. As Bali celebrates Nyepi, life stands still and quietude descends on this one-of-a-kind 'Day of Silence'. The Balinese Hindus believe that before ushering in the New Year, one should meditate for self introspection, which can be achieved by observing a fast, and maintaining silence with very little movement inside the house and none at all outside – virtually closing the gates, switching off lights and having no fire for the day.

Navaratri: Navaratri ('nava' + 'ratri') literally means 'nine nights'. This ritual is observed twice a year, in spring and in autumn. 'Vasanta Navaratri' or Spring Navaratri is nine days of fasting and worship that Hindus undertake during spring every year during which the devout Hindu seeks the blessings of the mother goddess. The Divine Mother or Devi is worshipped during the Vasanta Navaratri. This occurs during the spring. She is worshipped by her own command.

Ramnavami: Ramnavami or the birthday of Lord Rama falls on the 9th day of the bright fortnight of the month of Chaitra (March-April). In honour of Lord Rama Ramnavami, it is one of the most important festivals of the Hindus, particularly the Vaishnava sect of the Hindus. On this auspicious day, devotees repeat the name of Rama with every breath and vow to lead a righteous life. People pray to attain the final beatitude of life through intense devotion towards Rama and invoke him for his blessings and protection.

Dionysian Festival: The Greek Dionysian festival was known as Great Dionysia or City Dionysia. This festival is highly significant as the origin of dramatic tragedy and comedy. The Great Dionysia is thought to have been founded, or at least revived, by the tyrant Pisistratus (c. 530 BCE). It was held in Athens at the end of March, when the city was once again full of visitors after the winter. The festival honoured Dionysus Eleuthereus, who was said to have been introduced into Athens from the village of Eleuterae.

Meditation

Take a deep breath in through your nose and a long sigh out through your mouth. Feel any tension in your body start to melt away as you become comfortable and relaxed. Take another breath in through your nose, the air going deep into your stomach, then slowly and gently release the breath out through your mouth.

Your everyday thoughts and worries fade away as you bring your attention solely to your breath as it moves gently in and slowly out. The world around you starts to dissipate and as it slips away you open your mind's eye to find yourself at the foot of a mountain. It's the beginning of spring when the air starts to get a little warmer and the snow that covered the fields is now only visible in patches where the sun hasn't yet touched. The mountain above you draws your attention. It is almost calling to you, and so you answer the call and start to walk towards it. As you approach the foot of the mountain you find a cloak on a boulder and decide to put in on as it will be colder on the way up. You start your climb.

The going is fairly easy to begin with. Bird song fills the air and the buttercups and daisies nestle in the grass that you are walking on. The ground starts to become a little rockier and the climb becomes a little steeper. You also notice that the air is cooler and so you pull your borrowed cloak around you. Although chilly, the air around you is clean and fresh. You stop to take a couple of big, deep breaths, filling your lungs with the crisp mountain air. It is so refreshing that it spurs you on to continue your climb.

Big rocks and boulders mark your way now. The plants that line your path are now alpines and heathers and gorse. You finally reach the top of the mountain and the view almost takes your breath away…you can see for miles and you feel as if you are standing on top of the world.

You become aware that you are not alone on the mountain top as a woman comes to join you in admiring the view. She is very ethereal and almost blends in with the mountain air. She speaks to you and her voice is very faint, nearly getting carried away on the breeze, but as you listen very carefully you begin to hear her clearly. She is giving you a message and you realise that this is your March goddess.

As she finishes her message she gives you a gift as a reminder. You thank her and in the blink of an eye you are alone again on the mountain. You feel the meditation starting to slip away as you begin to join the real world again.

You become aware of your breath. Take a deep cleansing breath in and a long sigh out, wiggle your toes, wiggle your fingers and when you are ready open your eyes.

Take as long as you need to come back into the room. Write down any messages you were given on your journey.

Energy/Spell Work

The month of March heralds the spring and the celebration of Ostara, so magical workings for this month are:

- New beginnings
- Rebirth
- Renewal
- New life
- Growth

- Balance
- Fertility (not just for babies! Fertility in new projects and ideas too)
- Reconciliation
- Resolving issues and conflicts
- Protection
- Self control
- Communication

Moon Lore

Our ancient ancestors tracked the passing of time by the phases of the moon. The full moon marking the start of the month, or moonth, and each lunation lasting approximately 29 days. Gradually each moon was given a name or a label, as we humans like to do. These names would be dictated by what was happening weather wise, such as Wind Moon, or what activities were taking place – Seed Moon, for example. Unfortunately, there is no definitive list of names we can give, but throughout this course we will provide examples and more importantly we invite you to create your own list of names.

The March brings the Wind Moon and with it energies of transformation, rebirth and balance. Light wins the fight over darkness and you can start to really feel the heat from the rays of the sun. Let the March winds blow away the staleness of winter and help us to release that which we no longer need.

Names for the March Moon Include
Chaste Moon, Wind Moon, Worm Moon, Seed Moon

In the Celtic Tree Calendar
Ash Moon: 18th February-17th March; travel, transformation, spiritual journeys
Alder Moon: 18th March-14th April; balance and fertility

During this month's full moon go outside if you can and soak up her energies, let her speak to you and see what names come to you.

Ritual
We believe that personal rituals should be…well personal! So we have given you an outline guide for your own ritual, but it is up to you to invoke the deity/deities of your choice. Ones relevant to this month would be good because that's the idea of this course, but if someone else is shouting 'pick me, pick me' don't ignore them. Add in your own individual ideas and style and make the ritual your own.

- Cast the circle
- Call in the quarters
- Invoke deity
- Smudge
- Work some magic or divination or just sit quietly and meditate
- Feast…
- Thank and dismiss the quarters
- Thank and bid farewell to deity
- Close the circle
- And don't forget to ground!

Crystals
Crystals have often been associated with each month and/or the magical energy that the month brings. Try popping one in your pocket, on your altar or meditate with one this month. Again go with your intuition but here are some to get you started:

- Aquamarine
- Bloodstone
- Hematite

- Imperial topaz
- Ruby
- Amethyst
- Pink fluorite
- Anyolite
- Aventurine
- Carnelian
- Citrine
- Diamond
- Fire agate
- Kunzite
- Lodestone
- Pink tourmaline

Our Favourite Gem for March – Ruby
Ruby carries a powerful energy and is thought to be a life force and life blood conduit. It helps bring a zap of energy, but also helps to help increase your circulation and energy levels in general.

Ruby can be used to help release anger or negative energy.

Used in the home, ruby brings protection for your house, family and belongings.

Wear ruby to stop nightmares and to bring prosperity and success your way.

Crystal Grid
You could use the energies of this month to make a crystal grid. Start with a crystal in the centre and add your intent, if it is for business success you could put a business card under the centre crystal then add crystals going around in a spiral or a mandala pattern fanning out from the centre. I like to add herbs and oracle or tarot cards to my crystal grids too. Once your intuition has told you what crystals to use and where to put them, visualise all the crystals, herbs and cards linking up with a 'web' of white light to

bring your intent to reality.

Oil/Incense Blends

Create an essential oil or a loose incense blend to use when you are meditating or just to help you work with the energies of this month. Here are some herbs and scents for incense that we associated with this month, but go with your own ideas:

- Lotus
- Magnolia
- Ginger
- Jasmine
- Rose
- Sage
- Lavender
- Narcissus
- African violet
- Ginger
- Broom
- Strawberry
- Ginger
- Star anise
- Catnip

Our Favourite Herb for March – Broom (Cytisus scoparius)
This is a sturdy shrub with long green branches covered with yellow flowers in early summer followed by seed pods.

If you can get hold of several branches of broom you can tie them together to make a symbolic broom to use for sweeping away negative energies in your home or around the circle in ritual and bringing in protection.

Broom can also be used for wind magic – either to calm the winds or whip one up.

The flowers are considered lucky and also protective if worn or carried.

Essential Oil/Incense Recipe – Blustery Days Incense
Mix together:

> 3 parts cedarwood
> 2 parts parsley
> 1 part dried lemon peel

Altar

We would love for you to create an altar for the month. Go with your heart, but think about what this month means to you, what the weather is like, what the magical energy represents and if a goddess came to you then a representation of her would be good too.

Perhaps give your altar a real new beginning feel with brightly coloured painted eggs, symbols of lambs, rabbits and chicks and maybe even some chocolate...

Mandala

Mandala is a Sanskrit word meaning circle and is a spiritual and ritual symbol that represents the universe. A mandala will often have a square with four gates containing a circle with a centre point, but there are many variations.

Working with mandalas, whether you draw your own or colour in one that has already been created, can be a very relaxing and a surprisingly meditative exercise. You can find lots of free mandalas to download on the internet and colour, but also have a go at creating your own mandala for this month or for a particular goddess.

Pop on some quiet music, get your crayons out, release your inner child and allow yourself to be drawn into the mandala creation...you might be surprised what inspirations you find...

Once your mandala is finished, pop it on your altar.

Spirit Doll

Spirit dolls, poppets, goddess dolls...lots of different names from different cultures, but we thought it would be interesting to create a spirit doll, poppet or goddess representation for each month. Use whatever materials you have to hand or find easiest to work with – felt, cloth, string, Fimo, modelling clay...get creative.

Channel the energy of this month into your creation or add the characteristics and symbols of your chosen goddess.

If you make a doll from felt or material you can add herbs, spices and crystals to the inside too. If you work with clay or Fimo you can also incorporate herbs and crystals into the design.

The finished dolls will carry your very own magical energy with them together with the spirit of the month or the goddess you intended. Keep them on your altar.

Goddess Beauty

Green Tea Sugar Scrub

125g (4½oz) granulated sugar
2 green tea bags (1 to brew and one to open)
2 tablespoons coconut oil

Place one of the green tea bags in a couple of tablespoons of boiling water and allow it to brew. Meanwhile, in a bowl combine the sugar, coconut oil and the loose tea from the other teabag. Then once the brewing tea has cooled a little begin to add it to the mix a little at a time. The texture should end up a little like wet sand. You can make it grainier or wetter depending on preference.

Use the scrub in the bath or shower straight away or seal it in a container with a tight fitting lid. The scrub should keep for a couple of days, but is not long life.

Goddess Gift

The divine provides us with gifts...and we encourage you to step outside and see what the goddess, the divine, Mother Nature, has gifted you with.

It might be a feather, a pebble, a shell or maybe a leaf from a tree. Whatever you are gifted with you can add to your altar or maybe, if you are feeling artistic, you could create something with it.

A twig becomes a wand, a shell becomes a pendant, a feather becomes a smudge fan...think outside the box.

Medicine Bag

We have goddess medicine bags that we work with, just a square of material tied with a piece of thong, but inside we have representations of each goddess we have worked with. It helps us to keep a record of our journey, but also provides a focus for meditation and spiritual workings.

If you would like to create your own you can use a square of fabric. A bag made from felt or fabric works well too.

Each time you work with a different goddess ask them what symbol you should use to represent them in your medicine bag...you may be surprised.

By the end of this course you will have a wonderful collection of spiritual goddess items to keep in your own medicine bag.

Meditation Beads

Your mind can sometimes tend to wander when you are meditating, which leads to a loss of concentration. For practising meditation, meditation beads can act as a kind of 'anchor', or grounding point, enabling you to focus better. This can be extremely useful, especially if you are feeling tired when you meditate.

Conversely, if your mind is too active and over-energised, meditation beads will prevent you from becoming distracted or daydreaming. And, because the beads are moved in rhythm with your breathing, it helps you maintain your concentration.

At the end of this course you should have your own set of personal deities so you could create a string of meditation beads using one bead for each of your deities. It could be in the form of a necklace containing a bead for each of your twelve goddesses or you could make individual bracelets or pendants, one for each month.

The beads don't need to be used solely for meditation, you can use them throughout the day. When you awake, hold the beads and run them through your fingers and connect with their energy. This will set you up with positive intentions for the day.

Carry the beads with you in your pocket or bag, take them out during the day to remind you to stay grounded and focus on your tasks. Trust me, I need these all the time for focusing!

Hold the beads when you feel stressed or spacey to help bring you back centred and calm.

Finish your day the way you started by running the beads through your fingers and count your blessings. Release the negative points from your day and allow them to be replaced by the positive. Feel the good energy from the fabulous points of your day wash over you.

You also don't need to spend huge amounts of money. There are some beautiful meditation beads out there (often called prayer beads or malas), but you can make them yourself with whatever beads you have. There is no need to create a set of beads using expensive natural stones (although they are beautiful and full of natural energy). If all you have are wooden or plastic beads then use them, raid your children's play box even! The idea of the beads is to use them as a focus so even if you have a string of dried peas the intention is the same.

Feasting

We have included a recipe for each month – basically we don't need any excuse to include a cake recipe...but if you feel inclined to pop into the kitchen to bake we have given monthly suggestions on cakes to use in ritual to honour the goddess or just because they are yummy. If you love to cook you don't have to stop at cake, you could create a meal in honour of the goddess you are working with for the month (or just order a takeaway).

Chocolate Brownie Chocolate Meringue Cake
Complete chocolate and sugar overload...

4 egg whites
250g (8oz) caster sugar
Large tub double (heavy) cream
½ teaspoon vanilla extract
Chocolate buttons, chocolate sweets
Chocolate brownies (see recipe below)

Preheat the oven to 140C/275F/Gas 1.

Draw two 8 inch circles on two sheets of baking parchment and place on two baking trays.

Whisk the egg whites until stiff then add in the sugar gradually one spoonful at a time, whisking continuously until the mixture is stiff and glossy. Pipe the meringue in a spiral inside the marked circles on the baking parchment to create two 8 inch spirals.

Bake the meringue rounds in the oven for 1-1¼ hours until crisp and dry. Leave them to cool then carefully peel away the baking parchment.

Whip the double cream with the vanilla extract until thick.

Lay one of the meringue discs onto a serving plate and spread or pipe half the double cream over it.

Sprinkle with chopped chocolate brownies, chopped chocolate pieces, chocolate buttons or whatever chocolate sweets you like over the cream. You can even drizzle some melted chocolate over it too. Place the second meringue disc on top. Pipe or spoon the remaining whipped cream on top. Decorate with more chopped chocolate brownies and chocolate sweets.

You can use shop-bought chocolate brownies as you will only need two or three brownies, but I used the recipe from our *Cakes from the Cauldron* cook book and had some left over to eat. The recipe follows.

Chocolate Brownies

    200g (7oz) dark chocolate, roughly chopped
    175g (6oz) butter
    325g (11½oz) sugar
    130g (4½oz) plain (all purpose) flour
    3 eggs

Preheat the oven to 170C/325F/Gas 3.

Put the chocolate and butter in a bowl over a saucepan of simmering water until melted and smooth (or use the microwave). Add the sugar into the chocolate mixture and stir well. Add in the flour and stir until incorporated. Then stir in the eggs and mix until thick and smooth.

Pour into a lined 33 x 23cm baking tin.

Bake for 35-45 minutes. The top of the brownie should look flaky, but will still be slightly soft in the centre.

Leave to cool completely before slicing.

April

Drip drop drip little April showers… April can be a bit hit and miss with the weather, but it is (usually and hopefully) most definitely spring. Plants are starting to really come alive, the seeds planted at Ostara are making good headway and the weather is (she says again hopefully) a bit warmer.

We are working off the back of the spring equinox and heading towards Beltane, everything is alive and buzzing with energy.

I think the equinox always brings about changes of one kind or another (in my experience anyway). It is a time to clear out the old and that which has not worked and to bring in new projects, new ventures and new ways of thinking, make changes that bring in the positive. It is so easy to get caught in a cycle of destructive or unhealthy actions, now is the time to break free (yep I am singing now…). Sometimes we end up taking on too much then finding our entire life is out of balance and it has a ripple effect, like dropping a pebble into a still pool. The ripples from one tiny stone can have a huge effect on everything else. The equinox gives us an opportunity to rebalance and use all the energy that Beltane brings with it to put those changes into action.

Take a step back…take a really good look at your life and see where you can make changes to bring it back into alignment, to give a good balance between work, friends, family, play and 'you' time. Even little changes are a start and can lead onto bigger ones.

Deities
In this part of the course we suggest nine goddesses that we associate with this month. Have a read through the information and see if any of them resonate with you. It may be that one of them comes to you in the meditation, it might be that another deity altogether greets you…go with your intuition. We have also

included a list of some deities that have celebrations or feast days within this month too.

Calliope
Cailliope is a Greek goddess of eloquence. She is the eldest of the nine Muses and her talent is that of poetry. If requested she will bring anyone seeking it – creativity and the power of beautiful wordery. She can bring inspiration in the form of music, song writing and the confidence to perform.

Sarasvati/Saraswati
She is a Hindu goddess of words. Sarasvati is the creator of all the arts including music, dancing and poetry. She also created science and maths and invented the Sanskrit language, so she rules all aspects of teaching and learning. She is 'the flowing one' who can inspire anyone who wishes to follow her to increase or inspire their creativity and poetic or musical abilities.

Erzulie
Erzulie is a West African goddess and is the spirit of love, beauty, jewellery, dancing, luxury, and flowers. Gay men are considered to be under her particular patronage, as are prostitutes. She wears three wedding rings, one for each husband – Damballa, Agwe and Ogoun. Her symbol is a heart, her colours are pink, blue, white and gold, and her favourite offerings include jewellery, perfume, sweet cakes and liqueurs. Coquettish and very fond of beauty and finery, Erzulie is femininity and compassion embodied, yet she also has a darker side; she is seen as jealous and spoiled and within some Vodoun circles is considered to be lazy. Follow her and stay in her favour and you will never want again…cross her and you will suffer her wrath…

Blue Tara
A Tibetan goddess of liberation, Tara is worshipped in many

forms throughout Eurasia and in Hinduism and Buddhism. As Blue Tara she liberates humanity from emotional obstacles as well as worldly boundaries. She is the protector who destroys negative aspects of life in order to embrace the positive.

Hathor

She is the daughter of Ra, and an Egyptian goddess symbolising love, music and sexuality; the embodiment of success and abundance. She is the patroness of dancers and musicians and rules all aspects of womanhood and femininity. Hathor bestows happiness and joy on her followers. She was considered to be mother to all the pharaohs. Her talents also include the knowledge of every child's destiny. Traditional offerings to her include two mirrors and myrrh.

Seshat

Seshat created hieroglyphics and is not only an Egyptian goddess of writing, but also rules the written word in all its various forms. She invented calculations and measurements and in this guise she is the patroness of accountants (well someone has to be...) and architects. She is also a protector of books and a goddess of history. All kinds of writing implements from pens to scrolls are sacred to her.

Ma'at

The Egyptian goddess of truth, law and justice. She holds the scales in the Hall of Two Truths. Every pharaoh was considered to be beloved of Ma'at. She is a pillar of society and can bring about justice and balance. She carries divine order, truth, traditions, customs and morals with her.

The Valkyries

Messengers of Odin and Norse goddesses of the dead, they are a group of beautiful shape-shifting goddesses leading the dead warriors to the afterlife. With warrior spirit, they also control the elements.

Ushas
Ushas rides a chariot across the sky every morning bringing light to the world; she is a Hindu goddess of the dawn and gives potential and spiritual enlightenment to those who seek it from her. She also protects against evil.

Feast/Celebration Days
We have listed here the feast and celebration days for deities (we have included gods as well as goddesses) throughout April from various cultures and pantheons. These are taken from our own research…we apologise for any errors, but history is a fickle thing and calendars have changed over the years.

1st April
Venus/Fortuna/Concordia: The goddess Concordia was invoked with Venus and Fortuna by married women at the Veneralia on 1st April. At the time when Venus was worshipped the first day of the month was a festival in her honour and it was customary to play all sorts of pranks to do her veneration.
Fortuna Virilis: This festival was celebrated by women who wished to improve their relationships with the men in their lives. Also it was a festival during which select women of Rome gave the statue of Venus its yearly ritual bath.
Egyptian Festival of Renenutet: Also identified as the birthday of Nepri (personification of grain).

4th April
Megalesia/Cybele: The Megalesia was a festival in honour of the Magna Mater (Cybele) celebrated annually on 4th April with processions and games. The Megalesia, the Festival of the Great Mother, began with a ceremonial offering of herbs at the temple

of Magna Mater followed by her priests carrying her cult statue through Rome, accompanied by tambourine and cymbal players. The priests were blood-stained by wounds inflicted upon themselves. During the festival there were games in the Circus Maximus, theatre performances, sacrifices, and feasts. The last day of Megalesia featured horse racing.

5th April

Kybele: According to the Sibylline oracle, the holy stone image of Kybele was received at Ostia by the first citizen of the land, an honour accorded to Scipio Nasica and carried by the most esteemed matrons to the Palatine where, hailed by the cheers of the multitude and surrounded by fumes of incense, it was solemnly installed. A temple was erected to her on the summit of the Palatine and every year a celebration enhanced by scenic plays commemorated the date of dedication of the sanctuary and the arrival of the goddess.

6th April

Delphinia: A festival celebrated in various towns in Greece in honour of Apollo surnamed Delphinius. He was assumed to be a wrathful god, so it was thought necessary to appease him. Seven boys and seven girls carried olive branches bound with white wool into the Delphinium.

7th April

Guan Yin: One of the most popular and well known female goddesses in Asia and probably in the world, Guan Yin is the Bodhisattva of Great Compassion in Mahayana Buddhism and also worshiped by Taoists. The 7th of April is acknowledged as her birthday. In most Buddhist monasteries, there is a Guan Yin hall dedicated to her. There are also many temples dedicated to her and they are usually called Guan Yin Temple, with her sculpture occupying the central shrine. These temples can have

Buddhist or Taoist origins. There are also sintuas (shrines) dedicated in her honour where the spirit of Guan Yin is manifested through a spirit medium. Devotees pray to Guan Yin for help during crisis, for protection during difficult times of their lives and also as a sign of respect to her. While Guan Yin reaches out to help all beings, her ultimate aim is to help them towards their enlightenment.

10th April
Anubis: Adoration of the Egyptian god Anubis.

11th April
Festival of Min: A four-day Egyptian festival at the new moon, according to the great festival list in the temple for Ramesses III at Medinet Habu.

12th-19th April
Ceres: The Cerealia were games introduced at the founding of the temple of Ceres.

This was a private religious festival dedicated to Ceres. There were a few public festivities as well, including a chariot race and public games that doubled as the closing of the Megalesia. During these festivities, all participants were required to wear white. Private rituals usually included an offering of milk, honey, and wine to Ceres.

15th-19th April
Demeter: The Thesmophoria was a festival to Demeter as the founder of agriculture and the civic rite of marriage.

15th April
Fordicalia/Tellus Mater: The festival of the Italian deity of Mother Earth was held on 15th April to ensure plenty during the year and was celebrated under the management of the pontifices

and the Vestal Virgins. During this festival a pregnant cow was sacrificed to Tellus Mater, 'Mother Earth', who was considered to be pregnant with seeds. The unborn calf was taken to the Grand Vesta in Rome, where the priestess of Vesta burned it in Vesta's sacred flame (considered to be the flame of the earth). The ashes of the burned foetus were kept safe for later use during the Parilia.

15th April

Baishakh: In mid-April, Bengalis usher in the new year with the Poila Baishakh celebrations, the Assamese in the northeast with Bihu festivals, and the Tamils in the south with Puthandu. Around this time, Hindus in Punjab get agog with Baisakhi, the springtime harvest festival marking the beginning of their new year, and the people of Kerala in the south of India welcome their new year – Vishu.

21st April

Pales: Festival for Pales, goddess of herds. During this festival, ritualistic cleansing of sheep/cattle pens and animals would take place. The shepherd would sweep out the pens and smudge the animals and pens with burning sulphur. In the evening, the animals were sprinkled with water, and their pens were decorated with garlands. Fires were started, and in them were thrown olives, horse blood, beanstalks without pods, and the ashes from the Fordicalia fires. Men and beasts jumped over the fire three times to purify themselves further, and to bring them protection from anything that might harm them (wolves, sickness, starvation, etc.). After the animals were put back into their pens the shepherds would offer non-blood sacrifices of grain, cake millet, and warm milk to Pales. The Parilia took place on the same day as the traditional day for the founding of Rome.

22nd April-1st May

Walpurgis/Thrimilci: The festival of Walpurgis, a Norse night both of revelry and darkness. The nine nights of 22nd April to 30th April are venerated as remembrance of the All Father's self-sacrifice upon the World Tree Yggdrasil. It was on the ninth night (30th April, Walpurgisnacht) that he beheld the runes, grasped them, and ritually died for an instant. At that moment, all the light in the nine worlds is extinguished and utter chaos reigns. At the final stroke of midnight, the light returns in dazzling brilliance, and the bale-fires are lit. On Walpurgisnacht, the dead have full sway upon the earth; it is the ending night of the Wild Hunt. The 1st of May is the festival of Thrimilci; the beginning of summer. Thrimilci is a festival of joy and fertility, much like Ostara; however, most of the northern world is finally escaping from snow at this time.

23rd April

Venus: There were two Vinalia festivals, on 23rd April, when the wine from the previous year was broached and a libation from it poured on the soil, and on 19th August. Both festivals are associated with the worship of Venus who as the goddess of gardens also had vineyards under her protection. It was also a special day for prostitutes, who paid homage to Venus.

25th April

Robigalia: A Roman festival intended to protect corn from blight. During Robigalia, in a special grove outside the city walls, offerings were given to Robiga. Rust coloured dogs and sheep were also sacrificed to him at the fifth milestone along the Via Claudia in order to ask for his help in keeping blight and mildew from entering the city limits.

28th April-3rd May

Flora: Originally Flora was a Sabine goddess of the spring and of flowers and blossoms to whom prayers were offered for the prospering of the ripe fruits of the fields and trees. She was also regarded as a goddess of the flower of youth and its pleasures. The Floralia was a theatrical feast and one of unrestrained merriment. There were many theatrical performances largely consisting of lewd farces called mimes. The people were regaled during the games with porridge, peas and lentils. Animals with great fertility (rabbits, goats, etc.) were released into the country. Women were encouraged to wear brightly coloured clothing, and wear flowers as garlands and in their hair during Floralia to honour Flora. The Floralia was also regarded as a festival for prostitutes.

30th April

St Walpurga: On Walpurgis night was the eve of May Day, when the old pagan world of witches was supposed to hold high revelry in certain high places. St Walpurga was a Sussex (UK) born woman saint who immigrated to Germany. Walpurg is an old Teutonic name for the Earth Mother.

End of April

Feriae Latinae – 'Feast of the Latin League': This festival honoured Jupiter Latiaris, and was one of the festivals appropriated from the Latins. It was held at Jupiter's temple on the Alban Mount. During the Feriae Latinae, milk and other agricultural foods were offered to Jupiter. A white cow that had never worked was sacrificed and eaten by representatives from all of the cities in the Latin League. The trees in the area were decorated with human-shaped puppets dangling from the branches. The Feriae Latinae was a one-day festival, but if anything went wrong the whole thing had to be repeated until it went perfectly. The feast was followed by two days of public games.

Akshaya Tritiya: Hindus believe in the theory of 'mahurats' or auspicious timings in every step in life – be it to begin a new venture or making an important purchase. Akshaya Tritiya is one such momentous occasion, which is considered one of the most auspicious days of the Hindu calendar. It is believed that any meaningful activity started on this day would be fruitful. Akshaya Tritiya falls on the third day of the bright half of Vaishakh month (April-May), when the sun and moon are in exaltation; they are simultaneously at their peak of brightness, which happens only once every year. Akshaya Tritiya, also known as 'Akha Teej', is traditionally the birthday of Lord Parasurama, the sixth incarnation of Lord Vishnu. People conduct special Pujas on this day, bathe in holy rivers, and make a charity, offer barley in a sacred fire, and worship Lord Ganesha and Devi Lakshmi on this day.

Meditation
Take a deep breath in through your nose and a long sigh out through your mouth. Feel any tension in your body start to melt away as you become comfortable and relaxed. Take another breath in through your nose, the air going deep into your stomach, then slowly and gently release the breath out through your mouth.

Your everyday thoughts and worries fade away as you bring your attention solely to your breath as it moves gently in and slowly out. The world around you starts to dissipate and as it slips away you open your mind's eye to find yourself standing on a mountain top. The view is stunning and it is as if you are standing on top of the world. You are admiring the view when a large bird comes into view. It is flying right for the mountain that you are standing upon. As it come nearer you see that there is a woman sat on the bird, she is riding it like a horse, complete with saddle. They draw closer to the mountain, close enough that the woman reaches out her hand and shouts for you to take hold.

You take her hand and she pulls you onto the magnificent bird's back and you are soon flying with her high above the clouds. The wind whips past you and you have no idea where you are headed, but you feel completely safe. The woman and bird are gliding along on the air currents, almost as if they are controlling them.

The woman speaks to you almost as if she can hear your thoughts and she tells you that she is the bringer of the breeze and she gives you a message just for you. You realise that this is your goddess of April.

As the goddess finishes her message you feel the bird start to make a descent as he glides so elegantly through the air and comes to rest at the edge of a meadow. As you climb down from the bird's back, the goddess gives you a gift as a reminder of your journey together. You thank her and the bird and they take to the air once more, leaving you on the ground at the bottom of the mountain.

You start to become aware of your breath as it slowly moves in and out. You slowly become aware of your surroundings again and give your fingers and toes a wiggle.

Take your time and open your eyes when you are ready, make a drink, eat some chocolate (or other food if you cannot eat chocolate) to ground, then journal the message the goddess gave you.

Energy/Spell Work
Energies to work with for spells in April are:

- Creating
- Producing
- Return to balance
- Change
- Self confidence
- Self reliance
- Opportunities
- Emotions
- Selfishness
- Transformation
- Manifestation
- Desires brought to reality

- Banish stubbornness
- Clearing blockages
- Releasing past personal issues

Moon Lore

Our ancient ancestors tracked the passing of time by the phases of the moon. The full moon marking the start of the month, or moonth, and each lunation lasting approximately 29 days. Gradually each moon was given a name or a label, as we humans like to do. These names would be dictated by what was happening weather wise, like Rain Moon, or what activities were taking place – Growing Moon, for example. Unfortunately, there is no definitive list of names we can give, but throughout this course we will provide examples and more importantly we invite you to create your own list of names.

The April moon has energies of openings and new growth. Be open to new possibilities, plant seeds both physically and spiritually to be nurtured by the growing warmth of the sun and the gentle April showers.

Names for the April Moon Include
Seed Moon, Growing Moon, Grass Moon, Rain Moon

In the Celtic Tree Calendar
Alder Moon: 18th March-14th April; balance and fertility
Willow Moon: 15th April-12th May; healing and expressing the emotions

During this month's full moon go outside if you can and soak up her energies, let her speak to you and see what names come to you.

Ritual
We believe that personal rituals should be...well personal! So we

have given you an outline guide for your own ritual, but it is up to you to invoke the deity/deities of your choice, relevant to this month would be good because that's the idea of this course, but if someone else is shouting 'pick me, pick me' don't ignore them. Add in your own individual ideas and style and make the ritual your own.

- Cast the circle
- Call in the quarters
- Invoke deity
- Smudge
- Work some magic or divination or just sit quietly and meditate
- Feast...
- Thank and dismiss the quarters
- Thank and bid farewell to deity
- Close the circle
- And don't forget to ground!

Crystals

Crystals have often been associated with each month and/or the magical energy that the month brings. Try popping one in your pocket, on your altar or meditate with one this month. Again go with your intuition, but here are some to get you started:

- Quartz
- Amber
- Aquamarine
- Azurite
- Carnelian
- Emerald
- Kunzite
- Kyanite
- Lapis Lazuli

- Rhodonite
- Rose quartz
- Selenite
- Tiger's Eye
- Variscite
- Diamond

Our Favourite Gem for April – Emerald
Associated with any ailments of the eye, it can help with healing. Emerald is a stone of youth and can also help the general health and energy levels for 'ladies over a certain age'...

Emerald is a very useful stone to have with you to help when giving birth.

It is a stone that brings protection in any situation, but particularly against abuse of all kinds.

Use emerald in ritual or magic work to help give your spell working a boost or to increase your psychic abilities.

Emerald works well to bring about prosperity, but also to keep your relationship stable.

Wear emerald to protect against psychic attacks and to banish nightmares. It is also an excellent stone to work with for past life recall.

Crystal Grid
You could use the energies of this month to make a crystal grid. Start with a crystal in the centre and add your intent, if it is for business success you could put a business card under the centre crystal then add crystals going around in a spiral or a mandala pattern fanning out from the centre. I like to add herbs and oracle or tarot cards to my crystal grids too. Once your intuition has told you what crystals to use and where to put them, visualise all the crystals, herbs and cards linking up with a 'web' of white light to bring your intent to reality.

Oil/Incense Blends

Create an essential oil or a loose incense blend to use when you are meditating or just to help you work with the energies of this month. Here are some herbs and scents for incense that we associated with this month, but go with your own ideas:

- Daisy
- Sweetpea
- Pine
- Bay
- Bergamot
- Patchouli
- Basil
- Dragon's blood
- Geranium
- Thistle
- Allspice
- Frankincense
- Fennel
- Musk

Our Favourite Herb for April – Dandelion (Taraxacum officinale)
We are probably all familiar with the dandelion, usually considered a weed, but it is incredibly useful for its medicinal properties and yummy as a salad leaf. Of course it has wonderful magical properties too.

Take a dandelion seed head and blow four times – once to each direction (north, east, south, west)…making a wish as you do so. I have also seen pretty little jars with dandelion seeds inside that are kept as 'wishing jars'.

Use dandelion seeds in abundance and love spells and workings. The dried flower heads are also good in psychic power incense blends.

A tea made from dandelion flowers is good to drink before

any divination work.

Incense/Oil Recipe – Spring Forward Oil
Mix together:

  3 drops mint
  1 drop lemon
  1 drop lavender

Altar

We would love for you to create an altar for the month. Go with your heart, but think about what this month means to you, what the weather is like, what the magical energy represents and if a goddess came to you then a representation of her would be good too.

Spring flowers and seeds are always good to decorate your altar with for this month.

Mandala

Mandala is a Sanskrit word meaning circle and is a spiritual and ritual symbol that represents the universe. A mandala will often have a square with four gates containing a circle with a centre point, but there are many variations.

Working with mandalas, whether you draw your own or colour in one that has already been created, can be a very relaxing and a surprisingly meditative exercise. You can find lots of free mandalas to download on the internet and colour, but also have a go at creating your own mandala for this month or for a particular goddess.

Pop on some quiet music, get your crayons out, release your inner child and allow yourself to be drawn into the mandala creation...you might be surprised what inspirations you find...

Once your mandala is finished, pop it on your altar.

Spirit Doll

Spirit dolls, poppets, goddess dolls...lots of different names from different cultures, but we thought it would be interesting to create a spirit doll, poppet or goddess representation for each month. Use whatever materials you have to hand or find easiest to work with – felt, cloth, string, Fimo, modelling clay...get creative.

Channel the energy of this month into your creation or add the characteristics and symbols of your chosen goddess.

If you make a doll from felt or material you can add herbs, spices and crystals to the inside too. If you work with clay or Fimo you can also incorporate herbs and crystals into the design.

The finished dolls will carry your very own magical energy with them together with the spirit of the month or the goddess you intended. Keep them on your altar.

Goddess Beauty

Turmeric Face Mask
Turmeric is a great antioxidant and so makes a wonderful ingredient to a facemask. It helps with eczema, acne, redness and inflammation as well as promoting healing and rejuvenation.

2 teaspoons turmeric
2 teaspoons honey
2 teaspoons milk or yoghurt

Put turmeric in a bowl and add the honey and then the milk/yoghurt. You can adjust the amount of milk you add to make sure you get a thick paste, you don't want the turmeric mixture to fall off your face as it will stain your clothes.

Make sure all make-up is removed and your face is washed and hair tied back. It might be an idea to wear an old T-shirt that won't matter if you stain it...just in case

Apply the mask evenly over your face. Try to get it beneath

the eyes as turmeric is great for reducing dark circles too! Leave the mask on to dry...probably about 20 minutes, before washing off with cold water.

Repeat the mask every few weeks if needed.

Goddess Gift

The divine provides us with gifts...and we encourage you to step outside and see what the goddess, the divine, Mother Nature, has gifted you with.

It might be a feather, a pebble, a shell or maybe a leaf from a tree. Whatever you are gifted with you can add to your altar or maybe, if you are feeling artistic, you could create something with it.

A twig becomes a wand, a shell becomes a pendant, a feather becomes a smudge fan...think outside the box.

Medicine Bag

We have goddess medicine bags that we work with, just a square of material tied with a piece of thong, but inside we have representations of each goddess we have worked with. It helps us to keep a record of our journey, but also provides a focus for meditation and spiritual workings.

If you would like to create your own you can use a square of fabric. A bag made from felt or fabric works well too.

Each time you work with a different goddess ask them what symbol you should use to represent them in your medicine bag...you may be surprised.

By the end of this course you will have a wonderful collection of spiritual goddess items to keep in your own medicine bag.

Meditation Beads

Your mind can sometimes tend to wander when you are meditating, which leads to a loss of concentration. For practising meditation, meditation beads can act as a kind of 'anchor', or grounding point, enabling you to focus better. This can be extremely useful, especially if you are feeling tired when you meditate.

Conversely, if your mind is too active and over-energised, meditation beads will prevent you from becoming distracted or daydreaming. And, because the beads are moved in rhythm with your breathing, it helps you maintain your concentration.

At the end of this course you should have your own set of personal deities so you could create a string of meditation beads using one bead for each of your deities. It could be in the form of a necklace containing a bead for each of your twelve goddesses or you could make individual bracelets or pendants, one for each month.

The beads don't need to be used solely for meditation, you can use them throughout the day. When you awake, hold the beads and run them through your fingers and connect with their energy. This will set you up with positive intentions for the day.

Carry the beads with you in your pocket or bag, take them out during the day to remind you to stay grounded and focus on your tasks. Trust me, I need these all the time for focusing!

Hold the beads when you feel stressed or spacey to help bring you back centred and calm.

Finish your day the way you started by running the beads through your fingers and count your blessings. Release the negative points from your day and allow them to be replaced by the positive. Feel the good energy from the fabulous points of your day wash over you.

You also don't need to spend huge amounts of money. There are some beautiful meditation beads out there (often called prayer beads or malas), but you can make them yourself with whatever beads you have. There is no need to create a set of beads using expensive natural stones (although they are beautiful and full of natural energy). If all you have are wooden or plastic beads then use them, raid your children's play box even! The idea of the beads is to use them as a focus so even if you have a string of dried peas the intention is the same.

Feasting

We have included a recipe for each month – basically we don't need any excuse to include a cake recipe...but if you feel inclined to pop into the kitchen to bake we have given monthly suggestions on cakes to use in ritual to honour the goddess or just because they are yummy. If you love to cook you don't have to stop at cake, you could create a meal in honour of the goddess you are working with for the month (or just order a takeaway).

Rhubarb and Ginger Cake

230g (8oz) rhubarb, chopped
30g (1oz) ground almonds
150g (5oz) unsalted butter
150g (5oz) brown sugar
30g (1oz) crystallised ginger, finely chopped
150g (5oz) self raising flour
1 teaspoon baking powder
2 large eggs, beaten

Preheat the oven to 190C and grease and line a loaf tin.

Beat the butter and sugar together until creamy, then add eggs a bit at a time along with a little flour to prevent the mix from curdling.

Beat in the rest of the flour, baking powder, ginger and ground almonds.

Next add the rhubarb.

Pour the mixture into the loaf tin and spread out evenly.

Bake in the oven for around 50 minutes until the cake starts to come away from the edges and a skewer pushed into the centre comes out clean.

May

And so begins the active part of the year; the earth is sending forth new life, the sap is rising, the birds are singing and growth is all around us.

This month is all about passion, power and raw energy, the fertility of new life and growth and the union of male and female energy in whatever form...nuddy prod games optional...

Everything you do in this month will bring you closer to your goals; use the energy that is all around you to focus your intent. Work with May's powerful, bawdy, raucous energy. Although it's not just about the animal instincts, this month also brings the magical properties of abundance and growth. It is time to work some magic to increase your bank balance and improve your health.

The 1st of May is Beltane or May Day and it is all about that *va va voom* passion; jump on board and get carried away with the fiery energy and make it work for you.

Don't forget to show some love for Mother Earth too...

Deities

In this part of the course we suggest nine goddesses that we associate with this month. Have a read through the information and see if any of them resonate with you. It may be that one of them comes to you in the meditation, it might be that another deity altogether greets you...go with your intuition. We have also included a list of some deities that have celebrations or feast days within this month too.

Corn Woman

A Native American goddess of sustenance, she is the personification of maize and the fertility of the earth. She is a triple goddess and grows from young to old eventually sacrificing herself so that her body may be absorbed by the earth to provide nourishment and seeds so that crops will grow to feed her people. Corn Woman teaches her followers how to pray and honour their deities properly as well as how to sustain health through the cultivation of food.

Green Tara

Tara is a Buddhist saviour-goddess especially popular in Tibet, Nepal and Mongolia. In Tibet her name is Sgrol-ma, meaning 'she who saves'. The mantra of Tara (om tare tuttare ture svaha) is the second most common mantra heard in Tibet, after the mantra of Chenrezi (om mani padme hum).

The goddess of universal compassion, Tara represents virtuous and enlightened action. It is said that her compassion for living beings is stronger than a mother's love for her children. She also brings about longevity, protects earthly travel and guards her followers on their spiritual journey to enlightenment.

Hera

('Hero'=defender.) Daughter of Kronos and Rhea, wife of Zeus and queen of the universe. Her jealousies and vengeances are legendary; not, perhaps, surprising in light of Zeus' proclivities. She is a patroness of the matronly virtues and a protector of womankind. Greek queen of heaven, Hera is the Olympian queen of gods and is the goddess of the sky, marriage and women.

Her symbols are the peacock, cuckoo and pomegranates.

Isis

Isis is the goddess queen of Egypt and is a goddess of magic and healing. She is also the patroness of women and children and protects marriage and vows of love. She uses her wisdom and sorcery to strengthen ancestral bonds and bring about change and transformation.

Mawu

Mawu is a West African moon goddess who rules the moon and the night sky and is honoured for the cool temperature she brings with her. She is the spirit of motherhood and shows her people how to celebrate and be guided by the wisdom of their ancestors. Her twin and consort is the sun god Liza and together they created the seven sets of twin deities who influence the world. The cowry shell is sacred to Mawu.

Juno

Juno is a goddess of marriage, pregnancy and childbirth. She is an embodiment of the traditional female roles of wife and mother. One of her titles was Lucino (meaning light) as she helped to bring children into the light of this world at birth. She was also said to set and strengthen a child's bones.

She is also a goddess of conception, a goddess to be called upon in labour and one who helps settle disagreements between spouses. Juno protected the finances of the Roman people. In this role she was the patron goddess of the royal mint. The month of June was named after her and it was considered the most favourable month to get married in.

Oonagh

An Irish queen of the faeries and a goddess of magic, glamour and illusion, she rules nature, devotion and relationships along with bringing the magic of the fae into your life. She is also a goddess of love and protector of young animals.

Gula

A patroness of physicians, this Mesopotamian goddess is one of healing – not just the physical healing but that of the complete body, mind and soul. She rules over all herbs and medicines and any chants or spells used for healing or health. She is, however, also the goddess of retribution, poison and sending illness to anyone who steps out of line...

Poluknalai
Lady of the beasts and a goddess from Afghanistan – she looks after all animals and nature; she is not only protector of all animals but also their creatrix.

Feast/Celebration Days
We have listed here the feast and celebration days for deities (we have included gods as well as goddesses) throughout May from various cultures and pantheons. These are taken from our own research...we apologise for any errors, but history is a fickle thing and calendars have changed over the years...

1st May
Beltane/May Day: It is time for the sun to rule over the summer. Beltane marks the passage into the growing season, awakening the earth and signalling a time of bounty. All the elements of a May Day celebration lead back to pagan celebrations – the May Queen wearing her hawthorn flower wreath to the May Pole itself. The May Queen represents the Norse goddess Freya. The May Pole is a symbol of fertility and weaving the web of life, jumping the Beltane fire would bring luck and fertility.
Feast for Lares Praestites: During the Roman Republic, the Lares Praestites were honoured on this day, especially at their temple on the Via Sacra.
Maia's Feast: Maia received the sacrifice of a pregnant cow on this day.
Danu/Danann: The Tuatha Dea Danann came to Ireland on Monday, the calends of May, in ships. The Tuatha Dea Danann signifies the people of the goddess Danu or Danann, who was the mother of gods.
Parasurama Jayanti: Lord Parasurama, also known as the 'axe-wielding Rama', was the sixth avatar of Vishnu, whose main

objective was to deliver the world from the oppression of the Kshatriya rulers or unrighteous kings who strayed from the path of dharma. Parasurama Jayanti, or the birthday of Lord Parasurama, is a major festival for the Brahmin or the Hindu priest class. On this day, devotees worship Parasurama and observe a ritual fast in his honour.

Bona Dea: The Good Goddess was an Italian goddess supposed to preside over the earth and all the blessings that spring from it. The anniversary of the foundation of her temple was held on the 1st May when prayers were offered to her for averting earthquakes.

Flora: Roman youths would apparently go into the fields and spend the kalends of May dancing and singing in honour of Flora, goddess of fruits and flowers. The Romans welcomed the month of May by dedicating the month to Flora. Roman children made images of Flora and decorated them with flowers on this day.

Maeve: A strong Celtic goddess, it is for Maeve that the hawthorn was named May or May-thorn. She became the goddess of Beltane in whose honour the May Queen was crowned. She is often referred to as Queen Mab/Maeve of the Faeries.

8th May

Flora: A popular Cornish (UK) festival was held annually on 8th May called 'the Furrey'. It is said to have been derived from the Roman Floralia in honour of the goddess Flora. People would parade the streets with garlands of flowers and dance. The name Furrey is possibly derived from the Latin word feria, meaning fair or holy day.

9th, 11th, 13th May

Lemuria: This is a private series of rites Romans held to ward off the Lemures (unwelcome family ghosts). For the rite, the pater familia (head of the household) got up at midnight wearing clothes without knots and washed his hands with pure water. He would then walk through the house without looking backwards, making the mano fico sign with his hand, spitting black beans out of his mouth and repeating a prayer nine times. After he was done, he would again wash his hands and would then make noise using instruments made of brass. It was thought that the Lemures would collect the beans instead of the souls of the living, and would be scared away by the noise. At the end of the rite he would again say a chant nine times and then look backwards to ensure that the Lemures were gone.

15th May

Sacrifice Day for the Tiber River: On this day the Vestal Virgins made a sacrifice to the River Tiber to convince it to bring a steady supply of water to the city of Rome for the rest of the growing season.

29th May

Ambarvalia: This purification festival was held to honour Ceres and Dea Dia. During the festival participants would walk around their fields to convince the gods to bless the growing plants.

30th May

Einherjar: Minor modern Asatru festival honouring the warriors who fell during battle and who ascended to Valhalla's halls.

31st May

Virgin Mary: The feast of Our Lady Queen of Heaven is kept on 31st May. Bread or cake is offered to the Virgin Mary on this day.

New Moon: The Egyptian Festival of the Valley was celebrated at the May new moon. This was the greatest festival of the Theban necropolis, when the image of Amun of Karnak on the east bank at Thebes was brought to the temples for the cult of individual kings on the west bank. A distinctive feature of this festival was the presentation of great quantities of flowers. This would have been a time for each family to feast with their dead, and the architecture and decoration of tomb-chapels at Thebes reflect such festive banquets

Full Moon – Vesta: Where the sacred fire of the moon was tended by Vestal priestesses, they were also responsible for rain rituals. The Vestal Virgins performed a ceremony at the May full moon to regulate the water supply.

Eleventh Day: Ekadasi in Sanskrit means 'Eleventh Day', which occurs twice in a lunar month – once each on the 11th days of the bright and dark fortnight respectively. Known as the 'Day of Lord Vishnu', it is a very auspicious time in the Hindu calendar and an important day to fast. According to the Hindu scriptures, Ekadasi and the movement of the moon has a direct correlation with the human mind. It is believed that during Ekadasi, our mind attains maximum efficiency giving the brain a better capacity to concentrate. Spiritual seekers are said to devote the two monthly days of Ekadasi in extreme worship and meditation, to make the most of its favourable influence on the mind. Religious reasons aside, these fortnightly fasts help the body and its organs get respite from dietary irregularities and over-indulgences. Lord Krishna says that if a person fasts on Ekadasi, 'I shall burn all sins. This day is the most meritorious day to kill all sins.'

Thargelia: Thargelia was a Greek festival of Apollo held in Athens on the 6th and 7th of Thargelion (late May). It was both a vegetation festival and a ritual expiation of communal guilt. The first day of the festival featured the cathartic rite of the pharmakos (scapegoat). One or two persons, male or female, were selected to be a scapegoat. They were usually criminals or outcasts, but occasionally an important person would sacrifice himself or herself for the city. The scapegoat was fed, led through town, and then expelled from the city. In times of severe calamity, the scapegoat might be thrown off a cliff, cast into the sea, or sacrificed on a funeral pyre. The rite of the pharmakos cleansed the town and prepared for the new harvest.

Meditation

Take a deep breath in through your nose and a long sigh out through your mouth. Feel any tension in your body start to melt away as you become comfortable and relaxed. Take another breath in through your nose, the air going deep into your stomach, then slowly and gently release the breath out through your mouth.

Your everyday thoughts and worries fade away as you bring your attention solely to your breath as it moves gently in and slowly out. The world around you starts to dissipate and as it slips away you open your mind's eye to find yourself at the gate of a little cottage. It is a typical chocolate box cottage with a beautiful garden full of spring flowers and herbs. It seems inviting so you make your way towards it. You open a little rickety gate and close it behind you. The path to the cottage is lined with lavender and tulips and there are bees buzzing around, darting in and out of the flowers.

In the corner of the cottage garden you see a lady picking plants from the herb garden. She sees you and beckons to you to come and help her. She hands you a basket of herbs and then you follow her as she disappears inside the cottage.

There is an open fireplace inside the cottage with a small fire set and a cauldron above it. The woman begins to chop up some of the herbs and places them in the cauldron to brew. You watch as she goes about her work and she indicates that you should chop the herbs in your basket too. As you both work she speaks to you and gives you a message. This is your May goddess...the healer.

Once the brew is ready she pours you a cupful of most delicious tasty tea you have ever had. Just a couple of sips makes you feel strong and ready to continue your journey. You thank the goddess for the tea and she gives you gift as you depart.

You leave the cottage and go back out of the garden gate. As you close the gate behind you, you become aware of your breath as it slowly moves in and out.

You slowly become aware of your surroundings again and give your fingers and toes a wiggle. Take your time and open your eyes; when you are ready, make a drink, eat some chocolate (or other food if you cannot eat chocolate) to ground and journal the message the goddess gave you.

Energy/Spell Work

May is a month to work with the powers of the element of fire and the passions of Beltane, but also to connect with the realm of Faerie.

Work magic this month for:

- Personal growth
- Wisdom
- Enlightenment
- Logic
- Emotions
- Banish bad habits
- Self esteem
- Personal goals
- Communication
- Sex magic
- Passion
- Unity
- Fertility
- Happiness

Moon Lore

Our ancient ancestors tracked the passing of time by the phases of the moon. The full moon marking the start of the month, or moonth, and each lunation lasting approximately 29 days.

Gradually each moon was given a name or a label, as we humans like to do. These names would be dictated by what was happening seasonally, like Flower Moon, or what activities were taking place – Harvest Moon, for example. Unfortunately, there is no definitive list of names we can give, but throughout this course we will provide examples and more importantly we invite you to create your own list of names.

May's moon brings forth bursts of life and sexuality. Fruit trees start to bloom and the world around you suddenly seems transformed into the Hanging Gardens of Babylon. It's time to rekindle the fire in your love life, dance, sing and make merry. This moon is also a good time for connecting with the fae and nature spirits.

Names for the May Moon Include
Hare Moon, Bright Moon, Dyad Moon, Flower Moon

In the Celtic Tree Calendar
Willow Moon: 15th April-12th May; healing and expressing the emotions
Hawthorn Moon: 13th May-9th June; fertility, love and prosperity

During this month's full moon go outside if you can and soak up her energies, let her speak to you and see what names come to you.

Ritual
We believe that personal rituals should be...well personal! So we have given you an outline guide for your own ritual, but it is up to you to invoke the deity/deities of your choice, relevant to this month would be good because that's the idea of this course, but if someone else is shouting 'pick me, pick me' don't ignore them. Add in your own individual ideas and style and make the ritual your own.

- Cast the circle
- Call in the quarters
- Invoke deity
- Smudge
- Work some magic or divination or just sit quietly and meditate
- Feast...
- Thank and dismiss the quarters
- Thank and bid farewell to deity
- Close the circle
- And don't forget to ground!

Crystals

Crystals have often been associated with each month and/or the magical energy that the month brings. Try popping one in your pocket, on your altar or meditate with one this month. Again go with your intuition but here are some to get you started:

- Amber
- Aquamarine
- Azurite
- Sapphire
- Carnelian
- Emerald
- Kunzite
- Kyanite
- Lapis lazuli
- Rhodonite
- Rose quartz
- Selenite
- Tiger's Eye
- Varisite
- Agate
- Citrine

- Chrysoprase
- Green tourmaline
- Hematite
- Serpentine

Our Favourite Gem for May – Azurite
This stone was said to be connected directly to the divine and has also been associated with the lost city of Atlantis.

Azurite can enhance and project your healing powers and help the life force flow properly through your body.

This stone can help ease worry, resolve communication issues, dispel gossip and overcome problems and blockages.

Work with azurite to bring you prophetic dreams and to communicate with the spirit world; it also works well for past life recall.

It is a good stone for professionals or those with leadership roles to carry.

Crystal Grid
You could use the energies of this month to make a crystal grid. Start with a crystal in the centre and add your intent, if it is for business success you could put a business card under the centre crystal then add crystals going around in a spiral or a mandala pattern fanning out from the centre. I like to add herbs and oracle or tarot cards to my crystal grids too. Once your intuition has told you what crystals to use and where to put them, visualise all the crystals, herbs and cards linking up with a 'web' of white light to bring your intent to reality.

Oil/Incense Blends
Create an essential oil or a loose incense blend to use when you are meditating or just to help you work with the energies of this month. Here are some herbs and scents for incense that we associated with this month, but go with your own ideas:

- Lilac
- Passionflower
- Rose
- Vanilla
- Birch
- Rosemary
- Almond
- Angelica
- Cinquefoil
- Frankincense
- Marigold
- Woodruff
- Apple
- Ash
- Bluebell
- Daisy
- Hawthorn
- Honeysuckle
- Ivy
- Meadowsweet
- Red clover
- Rose
- Rowan
- Sorrel

Our Favourite Herb for May – Honeysuckle (Lonicera caprifolium, Lonicera japonica, Lonicera periclymenum)
Apparently it was once thought far too dangerous to bring honeysuckle flowers into the house because the scent would cause young ladies to become 'unnecessary' and given to 'forbidden thoughts'...seems to me like a definite flower to keep indoors...

Dab honeysuckle oil on your forehead to promote quick thinking and boost your memory. This also helps to increase your psychic powers.

Use honeysuckle flowers in all prosperity and money workings.

Honeysuckle can be added to other herbs in magical workings to help balance the blend and aid in the effectiveness of the intent.

Use in incense blends to help you meditate, increase your psychic powers and connect with spirit.

Essential Oil/Incense Recipe – Keeper of the Flame Incense
Mix together:

2 parts dragon's blood
1 part dried orange peel
1 part clove

Altar

We would love for you to create an altar for the month. Go with your heart, but think about what this month means to you, what the weather is like, what the magical energy represents and if a goddess came to you then a representation of her would be good too.

Decorate your altar using male and female symbols and anything that says love and passion to you, along with representations of the element of fire.

Mandala

Mandala is a Sanskrit word meaning circle and is a spiritual and ritual symbol that represents the universe. A mandala will often have a square with four gates containing a circle with a centre point, but there are many variations.

Working with mandalas, whether you draw your own or colour in one that has already been created, can be a very relaxing and a surprisingly meditative exercise. You can find lots of free mandalas to download on the internet and colour, but also have a go at creating your own mandala for this month or for a particular goddess.

Pop on some quiet music, get your crayons out, release your inner child and allow yourself to be drawn into the mandala creation...you might be surprised what inspirations you find...

Once your mandala is finished, pop it on your altar.

Spirit Doll

Spirit dolls, poppets, goddess dolls...lots of different names from different cultures, but we thought it would be interesting to create a spirit doll, poppet or goddess representation for each month. Use whatever materials you have to hand or find easiest to work with – felt, cloth, string, Fimo, modelling clay...get creative.

Channel the energy of this month into your creation or add the characteristics and symbols of your chosen goddess.

If you make a doll from felt or material you can add herbs, spices and crystals to the inside too. If you work with clay or Fimo you can also incorporate herbs and crystals into the design.

The finished dolls will carry your very own magical energy with them together with the spirit of the month or the goddess you intended. Keep them on your altar.

Goddess Beauty

Herbal Foot Soak

This foot soak is great if you have tired feet from being on them all day. You will need a large bowl that is big enough to put both your feet in (and that you don't mind putting your feet in). Also you will need...

200g (7oz) Epsom salts
1 handful rose petals

1 handful mint leaves

2-3 slices fresh lemon

If you don't have these fresh ingredients you can substitute for a few drops of your favourite essentials oils.

Add the Epsom salts and fresh ingredients to your bowl, then fill it with warm water. Stir until the salts have dissolved. You can add a few drops of oil such as sweet almond if you have it to help moisturise.

Now it's time to pop your feet in and relax, maybe put on your favourite TV programme and have a glass of wine. Allow your feet to soak for a good 20 minutes to get the full benefit.

Goddess Gift

The divine provides us with gifts…and we encourage you to step outside and see what the goddess, the divine, Mother Nature, has gifted you with.

It might be a feather, a pebble, a shell or maybe a leaf from a tree. Whatever you are gifted with you can add to your altar or maybe, if you are feeling artistic, you could create something with it.

A twig becomes a wand, a shell becomes a pendant, a feather becomes a smudge fan…think outside the box.

Medicine Bag

We have goddess medicine bags that we work with, just a square of material tied with a piece of thong, but inside we have representations of each goddess we have worked with. It helps us to keep a record of our journey, but also provides a focus for meditation and spiritual workings.

If you would like to create your own you can use a square of fabric. A bag made from felt or fabric works well too.

Each time you work with a different goddess ask them what symbol you should use to represent them in your medicine bag...you may be surprised.

By the end of this course you will have a wonderful collection of spiritual goddess items to keep in your own medicine bag.

Meditation Beads

Your mind can sometimes tend to wander when you are meditating, which leads to a loss of concentration. For practising meditation, meditation beads can act as a kind of 'anchor', or grounding point, enabling you to focus better. This can be extremely useful, especially if you are feeling tired when you meditate.

Conversely, if your mind is too active and over-energised, meditation beads will prevent you from becoming distracted or daydreaming. And, because the beads are moved in rhythm with your breathing, it helps you maintain your concentration.

At the end of this course you should have your own set of personal deities so you could create a string of meditation beads using one bead for each of your deities. It could be in the form of a necklace containing a bead for each of your twelve goddesses or you could make individual bracelets or pendants, one for each month.

The beads don't need to be used solely for meditation, you can use them throughout the day. When you awake, hold the beads and run them through your fingers and connect with their energy. This will set you up with positive intentions for the day.

Carry the beads with you in your pocket or bag, take them out during the day to remind you to stay grounded and focus on your tasks. Trust me, I need these all the time for focusing!

Hold the beads when you feel stressed or spacey to help bring you back centred and calm.

Finish your day the way you started by running the beads through your fingers and count your blessings. Release the negative points from your day and allow them to be replaced by the positive. Feel the good energy from the fabulous points of your day wash over you.

You also don't need to spend huge amounts of money. There are some beautiful meditation beads out there (often called prayer beads or malas), but you can make them yourself with whatever beads you have. There is no need to create a set of beads using expensive natural stones (although they are beautiful and full of natural energy). If all you have are wooden or plastic beads then use them, raid your children's play box even! The idea of the beads is to use them as a focus so even if you have a string of dried peas the intention is the same.

Feasting

We have included a recipe for each month – basically we don't need any excuse to include a cake recipe...but if you feel inclined to pop into the kitchen to bake we have given monthly suggestions on cakes to use in ritual to honour the goddess or just because they are yummy. If you love to cook you don't have to stop at cake, you could create a meal in honour of the goddess you are working with for the month (or just order a takeaway).

Gooseberry and Almond Cake

    125g (4½oz) unsalted butter, softened
    200g (7oz) caster sugar
    3 large eggs
    75g (2½oz) plain flour
    75g (2½oz) ground almonds
    1 teaspoon baking powder
    350g (12oz) gooseberries, topped and tailed
    25g (1oz) flaked almonds
    1 tablespoon icing sugar

Preheat the oven to 190C/gas mark 5 and grease and line a cake tin.

Beat together the butter and 125g of the sugar until light and fluffy.

Add the eggs one at a time adding a tbsp of flour with each one to prevent curdling. Fold in the rest of the flour together with the almonds and the baking powder. Then pour the mixture into the cake tin.

Scatter the gooseberries with the caster sugar evenly over the cake mix and then pop into the oven for around 20-25 minutes. The gooseberries will sink to the bottom of the cake.

Sprinkle with almonds and return to the oven for about 10 minutes. Check the cake is cooked by inserting a skewer into it and it should come out clean.

Leave it to cool before removing from the tin, then dust with the icing sugar and serve.

June

June brings the height of summer and the good weather (we hope), midsummer, the summer solstice, the longest day and the shortest night of the year. We celebrate the end of a cycle that began at the winter solstice.

The word 'solstice' means 'standing of the sun' so take a moment to stop, just stand still and connect with the energy of the earth and the elements and energies that are all around you. Look back on your journey, back to the winter solstice and see what you have achieved, make a note of what worked and what didn't, how far you have come and acknowledge and celebrate your achievements, learning from any mistakes.

Count your blessings, celebrate and be thankful for what you have, spend time with your friends and family and get outside and enjoy nature in all its glory!

Deities
In this part of the course we suggest nine goddesses that we associate with this month. Have a read through the information and see if any of them resonate with you. It may be that one of them comes to you in the meditation, it might be that another deity altogether greets you…go with your intuition. We have also included a list of some deities that have celebrations or feast days within this month too.

Ceres
A goddess of grains, the harvest, agriculture and motherhood, she hails from Rome. Ceres teaches her followers how to work with the land and how to grow, harvest, store and prepare the food that she provides fertile and nourishing soil for. She is very much a 'hands-on' goddess liking to be involved in all the day-to-day adventures of her people. She is also a mother goddess,

showing her love and dedication to all the children within her care. She is often seen carrying a sceptre and a basket of fruit and flowers.

Kuan Yin

Chinese goddess of mercy and mother of compassion, she hears and responds to all prayers. She cares for the souls of the dead and relieves sinners from purgatory. Kuan Yin is the patroness of healers and can cure all kinds of ailments within the mind, body and spirit. Her name translates as 'she who hears the weeping world'.

Olwen

A Welsh goddess, she was the daughter of a giant. Her names translates as 'golden wheel' and she was also referred to as 'Lady of the White Tracks' because as she walked the pathway behind her would sprout with trefoil plants. She is also linked with faeries and can help with feminine power.

Amaterasu Omikami

Ruler of the heavens and Japanese sun goddess, she is the universe with her beauty and light producing fertile crops and showering her people with life.

Eurynome

A creatrix goddess from Greece, she emerged from the chaos before the world was created; she is the mother of all pleasure. She created all things by dancing to separate the water from the sky and the light from dark. She mated with a snake Ophion, who she created from the wind, and she gave birth to the Universal Egg from which all things grew.

Demeter

A Greek harvest goddess, she is mother of the seasons and

agriculture. She rules parenthood, sowing, ploughing and the abundance of the harvest. She will provide support during grief and suffering. She is the mother aspect in the triad with Persephone and Hecate. Often she is seen carrying a cornucopia filled with grains, vegetables and fruits.

Bhramari Devi
Hindu goddess of bees, her spirit resides in the heart chakra and emits the buzzing sound of bees. As such she is a great teacher for all the chakras. She is associated with bees, hornets and wasps, which cling to her body. She is often depicted as holding a mace, trident, sword and shield in her four hands.

Mary Magdalene
A Christian saint she is also seen as goddess of all feminine issues, strength, healing, sexuality, fertility and magic.

Senua
A British water goddess, she presides over sacred springs and rivers. She is also associated with good fortune and luck.

Feast/Celebration Days
We have listed here the feast and celebration days for deities (we have included gods as well as goddesses) throughout June from various cultures and pantheons. These are taken from our own research...we apologise for any errors, but history is a fickle thing and calendars have changed over the years...

1st June
Carna: This Roman festival is sacred to Carna, protective goddess of the physical body.

5th June
The Sheela-na-Gig/Damhnaid/Gobnet: The female saint

Damhnaid (possibly Domnu) had a place of worship in Ballyvourney in Cork, Ireland, where she was known as Gobnet. The bushes around the site were garnished with rags tied on by devotees. Near there was the holy well, the branches in the area were also hung with rags. The ritual consisted of devotees going four times around the cairn and saying seven prayers at each round. The Pattern, or festival day of Saint Gobnatt, was 5th June. Beggars assembled and exhibited a sheela, the image of a woman exposing the female genitals. Gyg is the name in Norse for giantess or goddess.

7th June

Callynteria and Plynteria: Feasts of adorning and cleansing were held on two days as a service of atonement held in Athens. The Erechtheum, sanctuary of Athena, was cleansed, the images unclothed and garments washed and the images purified.

9th June

Sigurdsblot: Norse festival honouring Sigurd (Sigifrith or Siegfreid), the great hero who slew the dragon Fafnir and won back the treasure of the Rhine.

Vestalia: The Vestalia was a festival in honour of Vesta, observed in Rome on 9th June. Banquets were prepared and meat sent to the Vestals to be offered to the gods, millstones were decorated with garlands as well as the donkeys that worked them. The matrons of the town walked barefoot in procession to the temple to ask for their households to be blessed and to make offerings. The millers and bakers all took the day off work.

11th June

Matralia: Matralia was a festival held in honour of the Roman goddess Mater Matuta. During the festival statues of the goddess were decorated with garlands and gifts by women who had been married once and cakes cooked in clay pots were offered to the goddess. Only one female slave was allowed into the temple on this day, the one chosen was then ritually slapped on the head.

12th June

Scirophoria: An annual Greek festival at the time of threshing. Priests and priestesses from the temples of Athena, Poseidon and Helios marched to the place known as Skiron under a large white umbrella, the umbrella symbolised protection of the soil from the sun.

14th June

Diipolia: A Greek festival held in Athens to honour Zeus as protector of the city. It was also called Buphonia from the sacrificed ox connected with it. A labouring ox was led to the altar of Zeus in the Acropolis, which was strewn with wheat and barley. As soon as the ox touched the consecrated grain he was punished by a blow on the neck from an axe delivered by a priest who instantly threw away the axe and ran... In his absence the axe was brought to judgement and condemned as a thing polluted by murder to be thrown in the sea. To kill a labouring ox, the trusty helper of man, was normally forbidden by custom. The sacrifice of one at this festival was exceptional.

15th June

Hapy and Amun: Offerings made to the Egyptian deities Hapy and Amun to secure a good flood.

20th/21st June

Summer Solstice/Midsummer/Litha: Midsummer is the longest day and the shortest night of the year. It is the height of the sun's power. Although the hot days of summer are yet to come, this is the point when the year starts to wane. At midsummer the goddess is heavy with pregnancy, just as the earth is pregnant with the coming harvest. For our ancestors, midsummer rituals focused on nurturing new life both in the ground and in the wombs (animal and human). The sun is at its peak in the sky, the sun god is at the peak of his life and we celebrate his approaching fatherhood.

Norse: The god Baldur is said to have been sacrificed at this time, but is reborn at Jul; the hero Sigurd was also said to have been slain by treachery at midsummer by his blood-brothers Hagan and Gunthur (Gundahar).

Wadjet: The Uraeus goddess Wadjet was believed to govern the 11th month of the Egyptian calendar (June).

Juno: The festival of Juno Moneta was held, Juno was believed to be the great guardian of the female sex.

Heras: A Greek 'day of all heras'. A hera is one who in the course of an earthly life has reached that single goal, achieving full communion with the Mother of all Things. A hera was often a guardian of a temple, community of village. (A hero was the male equivalent).

23rd June

Osiris/Ishtar/Isis/Tammuz: The rites of Ishtar and Tammuz were originally celebrated by the Mesopotamians at midsummer. Isis/Osiris or Ishtar/Tammuz festivals would have taken place in the Middle East during June/July.

25th and 26th June

Ludi Taurii/Ludi Taurei quinquennales: 'Games of the Bull'. These games were held every five years to honour and appease the Di Inferi (the gods below). They were held in the Circus Flaminius, and probably included bull fighting and sacrifices.

27th June

Initium Aestatis: This Roman festival celebrated the first day of summer and was sacred to Aestas.

30ᵗʰ June

Hathor: Eve of the Egyptian Hathor festival at Thebes.

Vesak Day: Vesak day is a Buddhist holiday commemorating the birth, enlightenment and death of the historical Shakyamuni Gautam Buddha. As there are diverse Buddhist cultures around the world, Vesak day is celebrated on different days by different traditions. On Vesak day, Buddhists visit monasteries to offer their prayers and to attend sermons led by Buddhist venerables. Buddhist prayers often extend beyond themselves to pray for world peace and harmony. They also perform rituals such as the bathing of the Buddha; a symbolic act to commemorate the devas and spirits who made offerings to the Buddha at the time of his birth. During the Vesak Day period, monasteries are decorated with Buddhist flags and flowers while vegetarian restaurants offer promotions as people abstain from meat as an act of compassion. Many Buddhist will also make donations to charity organisations and to free animals that are captured for human consumption.

Odunde Festival: Odunde means 'Happy New Year' in the language of the Yoruba people of Nigeria. A celebration of the African new year, the Odunde Festival centres on a vibrant procession where participants make offerings of flowers and fruit to the river goddess Oshun.

Meditation

Take a deep breath in through your nose and a long sigh out through your mouth. Feel any tension in your body start to melt away as you become comfortable and relaxed. Take another breath in through your nose, the air going deep into your stomach, then slowly and gently release the breath out through your mouth.

Your everyday thoughts and worries fade away as you bring your attention solely to your breath as it moves gently in and slowly out.

The world around you starts to dissipate and as it slips away you open your mind's eye to find yourself in a stunning meadow. It appears to be midsummer now and the meadow is full of summer flowers nestled in the lush green grass. Butterflies and bees are darting about, skipping from flower to flower. Birdsong fills the air and the warm summer sun is beating down on you.

You decide to take a little rest and so you find a place to sit down. You take off the cloak you have been wearing and spread it over the grass like a blanket. Then you sit or lay down to rest for a while.

The sun is warm, but there is a gentle breeze that caresses your skin. You notice the smells of the wild flowers and grass. You notice the rich smell of the soil as it is heated by the midsummer sun. As you take your rest a ladybird lands beside you, climbs a blade of grass and then flies away again.

In the distance you spot something under the trees at the edge of the meadow. You continue watching and from the woods emerges a beautiful woman on horseback.

She is coming straight towards where you are sitting and you stand up to greet her as she draws nearer.

This is the goddess of the meadow and your June goddess. Once she is close she dismounts and greets you. She holds out her hands to take yours and, as your palms touch, messages start to appear in your mind. You are a bit startled, but the goddess holds your gaze and smiles at you. You relax and listen to the inner messages.

The images stop and the goddess lets go of your hands then she reaches into the saddlebags on the horse and gives you gift. This gift will be a reminder of the message she gave to you.

She gets back on her horse and turns in the direction of the woods where she came from. As you watch her disappear you start to become aware of your breath as it slowly moves in and out.

You slowly become aware of your surroundings again and give your fingers and toes a wiggle.

Take your time and open your eyes when you are ready, make a drink, eat some chocolate to ground and journal all the messages the goddess gave you.

Energy/Spell Work

For the sunny month of June work with magic for:

- Faerie
- Communication
- Intuition
- Inspiration
- Intellect
- Movement of all sorts
- Creativity
- Transformation
- Banishing
- Manifesting
- Reaching your goals

Moon Lore

Our ancient ancestors tracked the passing of time by the phases of the moon. The full moon marking the start of the month, or moonth, and each lunation lasting approximately 29 days. Gradually each moon was given a name or a label, as we humans like to do. These names would be dictated by what was happening seasonally, like Rose Moon, or what activities were taking place – Mead Moon, for example. Unfortunately, there is no definitive list of names we can give, but throughout this course we will provide examples and more importantly we invite you to create your own list of names.

June's moon starts to bring everything you have worked for into fruition. It is the height of the growing season and the energy is at its full strength. Connect with the rhythms of the seasons, soak up the moonlight and feel fully alive and present in the moment.

Names for the June Moon Include
Mead Moon, Blessing Moon, Dyad Moon, Rose Moon

In the Celtic Tree Calendar
Hawthorn Moon: 13th May-9th June; fertility, love and prosperity
Oak Moon: 10th June-7th July; growth, success, blessings

During this month's full moon go outside if you can and soak up her energies, let her speak to you and see what names come to you.

Ritual
We believe that personal rituals should be...well personal! So we have given you an outline guide for your own ritual, but it is up to you to invoke the deity/deities of your choice, relevant to this month would be good because that's the idea of this course, but if someone else is shouting 'pick me, pick me' don't ignore them. Add in your own individual ideas and style and make the ritual your own.

- Cast the circle
- Call in the quarters
- Invoke deity
- Smudge
- Work some magic or divination or just sit quietly and meditate
- Feast...
- Thank and dismiss the quarters
- Thank and bid farewell to deity
- Close the circle
- And don't forget to ground!

Crystals
Crystals have often been associated with each month and/or the

magical energy that the month brings. Try popping one in your pocket, on your altar or meditate with one this month. Again go with your intuition, but here are some to get you started:

- Citrine
- Herkimer diamond
- Alexandrite
- Blue lace agate
- Emerald
- Jade
- Tiger's Eye
- Lapis lazuli
- Diamond
- Moonstone
- Pearl
- Turquoise
- Amber
- Carnelian
- Fire agate
- Green chrysoprase
- Moss agate
- Pink tourmaline
- Ruby
- Rhodonite

Our Favourite Gem for June – Citrine

Citrine is excellent to clear any negative energy from your home especially if you have some dark, shady and uncomfortable corners. It is brilliant for children to help relationships and to keep those lines of communication open (especially if you have teenagers...you know what I am talking about). Animals love citrine too; it helps them feel settled. Use citrine for protection against fear and negative energy.

Charge a piece of citrine with the intent of prosperity and

abundance and pop it in your purse to keep the money coming in.

Citrine can also help boost your intuition and focus on your inner knowing while aiding in all your psychic abilities. Use a piece of citrine to help visualise and ultimately achieve your dreams and goals.

To cleanse and recharge citrine leave it out in the sunshine especially this month on the summer solstice for an extra boost of juju.

Crystal Grid
You could use the energies of this month to make a crystal grid. Start with a crystal in the centre and add your intent, if it is for business success you could put a business card under the centre crystal then add crystals going around in a spiral or a mandala pattern fanning out from the centre. I like to add herbs and oracle or tarot cards to my crystal grids too. Once your intuition has told you what crystals to use and where to put them, visualise all the crystals, herbs and cards linking up with a 'web' of white light to bring your intent to reality.

Oil/Incense Blends
Create an essential oil or a loose incense blend to use when you are meditating or just to help you work with the energies of this month. Here are some herbs and scents for incense that we associated with this month, but go with your own ideas:

- Almond
- Dill
- Lily
- Lemongrass
- Clover
- Chamomile
- Cinquefoil

- Copal
- Elder
- Fennel
- Fern
- Frankincense
- Galangal
- Heliotrope
- Laurel
- Lavender
- Lemon
- Mistletoe
- Mugwort
- Oak
- Rose
- Sandalwood
- Thyme
- Verbena
- Wisteria
- Ylang Ylang

Our Favourite Herb for June – Clover (Trifolium pratense, Trifolium repens)

This is a common perennial plant with purple red or white flowers and small green leaves found growing on grassland and verges and flowering from late spring/early summer right through to autumn.

Clover is said to protect the virtuous against evil forces (well that's us scuppered then…).

An old poem from 1815 by Sir Walter Scott states: 'Trefoil, vervain, St John's Wort, dill, hinder witches of their will.' Trefoil is clover.

We all know that four leaf clovers are lucky. The three leaves are believed to represent faith, hope and charity (love) and the fourth was God's grace.

Clover flowers can also be carried with you to bring luck and success your way.

Essential Oil/Incense Recipe – Bountiful Land Oil
Mix together:

    3 drops rosemary
    2 drops lavender
    1 drop cypress

Altar

We would love for you to create an altar for the month. Go with your heart, but think about what this month means to you, what the weather is like, what the magical energy represents and if a goddess came to you then a representation of her would be good too.

Fill your altar with representations of the sun and sunshiny energy along with anything that makes you think of full on summer fun.

Mandala

Mandala is a Sanskrit word meaning circle and is a spiritual and ritual symbol that represents the universe. A mandala will often have a square with four gates containing a circle with a centre point, but there are many variations.

Working with mandalas, whether you draw your own or colour in one that has already been created, can be a very relaxing and a surprisingly meditative exercise. You can find lots of free mandalas to download on the internet and colour, but also have a go at creating your own mandala for this month or for a particular goddess.

Pop on some quiet music, get your crayons out, release your inner child and allow yourself to be drawn into the mandala creation...you might be surprised what inspirations you find...

Once your mandala is finished, pop it on your altar.

Spirit Doll

Spirit dolls, poppets, goddess dolls…lots of different names from different cultures, but we thought it would be interesting to create a spirit doll, poppet or goddess representation for each month. Use whatever materials you have to hand or find easiest to work with – felt, cloth, string, Fimo, modelling clay…get creative.

Channel the energy of this month into your creation or add the characteristics and symbols of your chosen goddess.

If you make a doll from felt or material you can add herbs, spices and crystals to the inside too. If you work with clay or Fimo you can also incorporate herbs and crystals into the design.

The finished dolls will carry your very own magical energy with them together with the spirit of the month or the goddess you intended. Keep them on your altar.

Goddess Beauty

Wild Rose Water
Rose is a natural astringent, tightens skin and reduces redness. It is used in a lot of beauty creams and lotions, but is fairly easy to make at home.

To get nice scent it is best to use wild roses as the modern cultivated ones are bred for their appearances rather than their scent. You should be able to find plenty of wild roses in hedgerows, parks and by wastelands. Pick the petals directly from the flower so you leave the hip place. If you can't get fresh petals then dried will work just as well or you could use lavender instead.

You will need about 15g of petals and double the amount of water.

Place the petals in a heat resistant bowl and cover with

boiling water. Cover the bowl with a lid or use a plate and allow it to steep for a good half an hour. After that time you can strain the water into a clean jar. Store the rose water in the fridge where it will keep up to a month.

You can use the rose water as a toner and apply it directly to your face on a cotton wool ball or pad. Or you can mix it into a cream or coconut oil and use as a moisturiser.

Goddess Gift

The divine provides us with gifts...and we encourage you to step outside and see what the goddess, the divine, Mother Nature, has gifted you with.

It might be a feather, a pebble, a shell or maybe a leaf from a tree. Whatever you are gifted with you can add to your altar or maybe, if you are feeling artistic, you could create something with it.

A twig becomes a wand, a shell becomes a pendant, a feather becomes a smudge fan...think outside the box.

Medicine Bag

We have goddess medicine bags that we work with, just a square of material tied with a piece of thong, but inside we have representations of each goddess we have worked with. It helps us to keep a record of our journey, but also provides a focus for meditation and spiritual workings.

If you would like to create your own you can use a square of fabric. A bag made from felt or fabric works well too.

Each time you work with a different goddess ask them what symbol you should use to represent them in your medicine bag...you may be surprised.

By the end of this course you will have a wonderful collection of spiritual goddess items to keep in your own medicine bag.

Meditation Beads

Your mind can sometimes tend to wander when you are meditating, which leads to a loss of concentration. For practising meditation, meditation beads can act as a kind of 'anchor', or grounding point, enabling you to focus better. This can be extremely useful, especially if you are feeling tired when you meditate.

Conversely, if your mind is too active and over-energised, meditation beads will prevent you from becoming distracted or daydreaming. And, because the beads are moved in rhythm with your breathing, it helps you maintain your concentration.

At the end of this course you should have your own set of personal deities so you could create a string of meditation beads using one bead for each of your deities. It could be in the form of a necklace containing a bead for each of your twelve goddesses or you could make individual bracelets or pendants, one for each month.

The beads don't need to be used solely for meditation, you can use them throughout the day. When you awake, hold the beads and run them through your fingers and connect with their energy. This will set you up with positive intentions for the day.

Carry the beads with you in your pocket or bag, take them out during the day to remind you to stay grounded and focus on your tasks. Trust me, I need these all the time for focusing!

Hold the beads when you feel stressed or spacey to help bring you back centred and calm.

Finish your day the way you started by running the beads through your fingers and count your blessings. Release the negative points from your day and allow them to be replaced by the positive. Feel the good energy from the fabulous points of your day wash over you.

You also don't need to spend huge amounts of money. There are some beautiful meditation beads out there (often called prayer beads or malas), but you can make them yourself with whatever beads you have. There is no need to create a set of beads using expensive natural stones (although they are beautiful and full of natural energy). If all you have are wooden or plastic beads then use them, raid your children's play box even! The idea of the beads is to use them as a focus so even if you have a string of dried peas the intention is the same.

Feasting

We have included a recipe for each month – basically we don't need any excuse to include a cake recipe...but if you feel inclined to pop into the kitchen to bake we have given monthly suggestions on cakes to use in ritual to honour the goddess or just because they are yummy. If you love to cook you don't have to stop at cake, you could create a meal in honour of the goddess you are working with for the month (or just order a takeaway).

Elderflower and Lemon Cake

> 225g (8oz) unsalted butter
> 225g (8oz) caster sugar
> 4 eggs
> 225g (8oz) self raising flour
> 1 teaspoon baking powder
> Splash of milk (if needed)
> Zest and juice of 1 lemon
> 100ml (3½fl oz) elderflower cordial (homemade is great, but I used shop bought)
> 2 teaspoons granulated sugar
> Round cake tin

Preheat the oven to 180C/Gas Mark 4.

In a bowl cream the butter, sugar and lemon zest together until light and fluffy.

Beat in eggs one at a time with 1 tablespoon of the flour to prevent curdling.

Add in the remaining flour. Add a splash of milk if the consistency is too stiff.

Pour the mixture into a cake tin and bake for 45-50 minutes until the cake is golden. Test by poking a skewer into the centre. If it is cooked, the skewer should come out cleanly with no cake mix on it. Once cooked, set the cake aside and allow it to cool for 5 minutes.

Meanwhile make your syrup topping. Squeeze lemon juice into a bowl and stir in the cordial.

Once the cake has cooled for 5 minutes, skewer it all over and pour on the syrup. This will seep into the tiny holes made with the skewer and leave you with a deliciously moist cake. Then sprinkle over the caster sugar and leave to cool completely.

July

In the summertime when the weather is hot…

What we often refer to as the height of summer, flowers are blooming, the skies are blue, there's not a cloud in the sky and hopefully it is warm.

Spend as much time outside as you can. I like to eat my lunch out in the garden and have spent many an evening sitting outside listening to all the sounds around me while sipping a cup of tea (or glass of wine) and chilling with friends and family as the sun goes down.

Still keep saving those flower petals and any seeds that start to appear, dry them and put them away for spell work later in the year.

Deities

In this part of the course we suggest nine goddesses that we associate with this month. Have a read through the information and see if any of them resonate with you. It may be that one of them comes to you in the meditation, it might be that another deity altogether greets you…go with your intuition. We have also included a list of some deities that have celebrations or feast days within this month too.

Sol

Norse goddess of the sun. Sol rides across the sky in a chariot every morning from east to west. The golden glow of her beauty and power warms and nourishes the earth.

Medb

Irish battle, hunter and warrior goddess who likes her drink and plenty of it, she also likes to take many lovers.

Durga

Definitely a protection goddess, the Hindu deity Durga has eighteen arms, rides a tiger and carries various weapons and sacred objects. She is a warrior, but also a mother goddess who teaches those who follow her to work with truth and receive love while also protecting them against all the negative and evil forces in the world. She destroys and attacks all those negative issues such as prejudice and jealousy and helps deal with egos and the sins of humans. She is one of immense power and shows just how to triumph over evil.

Sekhmet

Often referred to as the Eye of Ra, she is the personification of his anger. Sekhmet is an Egyptian goddess of punishment. She is both creative and destructive in her nature and represents the fire and power of feminine energy. She is a protector of woman, but also brings with her balance and the spark of righteous anger. She is often seen as a curvy lady with the head of a lion.

Ereshkigal

The goddess of Irkalla, the underworld kingdom, Ereshkigal is a Sumerian goddess of the underworld. She is the older sister to Innana/Ishtar. She is the darkness, the shadows, the unseen side of the unconscious, the ego and the soul. She rules the underworld totally and has the sole power to pass laws and give judgement.

Hestia

Hestia is daughter of Kronos and Rhea and a goddess of family life and the hearth. Her primary functions are patronage of hospitality to guests in an outward sense and family unity in an inward sense. Greek goddess of the hearth and home, as the goddess of the sacred flame, she is worshipped in the home where she provides protection, security, blessings and warmth.

Freya

A Norse maiden goddess of love and war, she is supposed to be the most beautiful goddess ever. No one, whether they are mortal or deity, can resist her. She is also the Queen of the Valkyries and in that guise gathers the souls of the dead and the slain warriors to escort them to the afterlife. Work with Freya for love, happiness and good family ties as well as any sexual or sensual issues. Her sacred day is Friday and her number is thirteen. She is also the mistress of cats and poetry.

Pele

The goddess Pele is a Hawaiian volcano and fire goddess. She is known as She Who Shapes the Sacred Land. Pele is passion, purpose, dynamic action and eternal and profound love. She will bring with her love, passion, creativity, motivation, energy, cleansing, renewal, fearlessness and also protection.

Belisama

An ancient Gaulish goddess, she came over to Britain with the Gauls and Romans. She is a solar goddess and she also rules rivers, the forge and crafts. She brings purification, strength and support in difficult times. Her name translates as 'bright summer'.

Feast/Celebration Days

We have listed here the feast and celebration days for deities (we have included gods as well as goddesses) throughout July from various cultures and pantheons. These are taken from our own research...we apologise for any errors, but history is a fickle thing and calendars have changed over the years...

1st July-middle of July

Rosalia: The Romans loved roses and used them whenever they could for festivals and special occasions. The feast of roses, the

Rosalia was a common event and held on dates ranging from 1st July to the middle of the month.

4th July

Aphrodisia: Greek festival in honour of Aphrodite, with sacrifices of a dove, myrtle tree, sea shells and roses. Dancing and athletic games took place.

12th July

Kronia: A harvest festival in honour of the god of agriculture, Kronos.

6th -13th July

Ludi Apollinares: 'Games of Apollo'. These games were first held in 212 BCE to celebrate Apollo as a god of healing (especially during war), and originally lasted for a single day (13th July). They were gradually expanded to eight days, with two days reserved for theatre performances, two days for games in the circus, and the remaining days for markets and fairs. Apollo was given sacrifices during the Ludi Apollinares, and all participants were expected to wear garlands while attending the events.

7th July

Nonae Caprotinae: 'Nones of the Wild Fig', also called 'Feast of the Serving Women'. This festival was held to honour Juno Caprotina, and a sacrifice was given to her under a wild fig tree. It also celebrates the serving women who helped free the city of Rome from the Gauls.

Parilia/Palilia: Festivals for Pales, goddess of herds. During these festivals, ritualistic cleansing of sheep/cattle pens and animals would take place. The shepherd would sweep out the pens and smudge the animals and pens with burning sulphur. In the evening, the animals were sprinkled with water, and their pens were decorated with garlands. Fires were started, and in were thrown olives, horse blood, beanstalks without pods, and the ashes from the Fordicalia fires. Men and beasts jumped over the fire three times to purify themselves further, and to bring them protection from anything that might harm them (wolves, sickness, starvation, etc.). After the animals were put back into their pens, the shepherds would offer non-blood sacrifices of grain, cake millet, and warm milk to Pales. The festival in April was for smaller livestock, while the one in July was for larger animals.

19th July

Feast of Opet: Every year during the second month of the floods came an Egyptian festival, for eleven days the capital celebrated the feast of Opet. Amun and his spouse Mut accompanied the god Khonsu in a ceremonial time of divine emergence, giving the crowds a glimpse of the triad of three great gods.

The Great Panathenaia: This Greek festival took place in July at the height of the summer heat when the need for rain was the greatest; the day of the festival was the birthday of the goddess Athena.

Aphrodite: At Alexandria the rites consisted of a huge pageant of the wedding of Adonis and Aphrodite.

23rd July

Neptunalia: This Roman festival celebrated Neptune as the god of irrigation. During the festival, participants would sit under arbours made from leaves. They would ask Neptune to continue supplying them with fresh water during the heat of the summer and early autumn. Salacia was also worshipped during the Neptunalia.

Athena: The Panathenaea, festivals in honour of the patroness of the Greek city of Athens, were first called Atheneaea. Originally they were observed on one day, but were eventually extended.

Four young virgins were yearly chosen from noble houses who then had to spend several months at the temple of Athena and take part in the services. Two of them had the task of commencing the cloak that the women of Athens wove and presented to the goddess. The other two, on the night of the festival, received from the priestess of Athena certain coffers with unknown contents that they carried in procession on their heads to a grotto beside the temple of Aphrodite of the gardens, receiving something in exchange, which they carried to the temple. Athena's procession garment was white and embroidered in gold with the achievements of the goddess. Her garment was hung upon the sail of a ship that was built for the procession, which upon reaching Athena's statue was placed upon her; the statue was then laid on a bed of flowers.

24th July

Isis-Neith: A feast of lamps was celebrated in Egypt in honour of Isis-Neith. The ceremony took place in an under chapel beneath the temple. Lamps were carried in procession around the coffin of Osiris.

25th July

Furrinalia: This festival venerated all those who searched for underground water sources. In Rome's early days it was a festival that took place in a grove on the Janiculum, and honoured the goddess Furrina.

Salacia: She was a Roman goddess of salt water and often regarded as wife to Neptune. A festival took place to her, where boughs were erected, possibly to bring blessings of sufficient water.

26th July

St Anne: Christian festival of St Anne, Mother of the Virgin Mary.

27th July
Hatshepsut: Festival of the Queen of Egypt and Priestess Hatshepsut, the only ruling female pharaoh of Egypt, who fostered exploration and the arts and cultivated government by peaceful means.

28th July
Pythias: Greek festival of Pythias, mother of Pythagoras.

29th July
St Martha: Palestinian festival of Martha, devoted to Jesus, revered by actions rather than words.

30th July
Mesut-Ra: Opening of the year, birth of Ra in Ancient Egypt.

31st July-1st August
Lithasblot: Norse harvest festival; giving thanks to Urda (Ertha) for her bounty. Often alms are given to the unfortunate at this time, or loaves in the shape of the fylfot (the sun-wheel, which fell into regrettable disrepute during the dark times of the Second World War when the symbol was perverted as a symbol of chaos and darkness). Lithasblot has long been associated with ceremonial magic and magical workings.

Rath Yatra: Hindu festival. Every year in mid-summer, Lord Jagannath, with his elder brother Balabhadra and sister Subhadra, goes on holiday, travelling on grand chariots, from his temple in Puri, to his garden palace in the countryside. This Hindu belief has given rise to one of the biggest religious festivals in India — the Rath Yatra or the Chariot Festival. This is also the etymological origin of the English word 'Juggernaut'. Jagannath, believed to be an avatar of Lord Vishnu, is the Lord of Puri — the coastal town of Orissa in eastern India. It is during this time that the three deities of Jagannath, Balabhadra and Subhadra are taken out in a grand procession in specially made gigantic temple-like chariots called raths, which are pulled by thousands of devotees. The festival begins with the Ratha Prathistha, or invoking ceremony, in the morning, but the Ratha Tana or chariot pulling is the most exciting part of the festival, which begins in the late afternoon when the chariots of Jagannath, Balabhadra and Subhdra start rolling. Each year these wooden chariots are constructed anew in accordance with religious specifications. The idols of these three deities are also made of wood and are replaced by new ones every twelve years. After a nine-day sojourn of the deities at the country temple amid festivities, the divine summer holiday ends and the three return to the city temple of Lord Jagannath.

Guru Purnima: The full moon day in the Hindu month of Ashad (July-August) is observed as the auspicious day of Guru Purnima, a day sacred to the memory of the great sage Maharshi Veda Vyasa. All Hindus are indebted to this ancient saint who edited the four Vedas, wrote the eighteen Puranas, Mahabharata and the Srimad Bhagavatam. Vyasa even taught Dattatreya, who is regarded as the Guru of Gurus. On this day, all spiritual aspirants and devotees worship Vyasa in honour of his divine personage and all disciples perform a 'puja' of their respective spiritual preceptor or 'Gurudevs'. This day is of deep significance to the farmers, as it heralds the setting in of the much-needed rains and advent of cool showers usher in fresh life in the fields. It is a good time to begin your spiritual lessons. Traditionally, spiritual seekers start to intensify their spiritual 'sadhana' from this day. The period 'Chaturmas' ('four months') begins then. In the past, wandering spiritual masters and their disciples used to settle down at a place to study and discourse on the Brahma Sutras composed by Vyasa, and engage in Vedantic discussions.

Adonia: During this moveable festival a household's female members would climb onto the roof of the house and plant the 'Garden of Adonis'. These gardens contained fast-growing plants. For eight days the women would tend to the plants, and then neglect them. After the plants had died the women would mourn for them. There was also a sacred play portraying the wedding of Adonis and Venus held during the Adonia, and was probably based on a Greek tradition. The last part of the festival involved making effigies of Adonis and placing them into coffins.

Meditation

Take a deep breath in through your nose and a long sigh out through your mouth. Feel any tension in your body start to melt away as you become comfortable and relaxed. Take another breath in through your nose, the air going deep into your stomach, then slowly and gently release the breath out through your mouth.

Your everyday thoughts and worries fade away as you bring your attention solely to your breath as it moves gently in and slowly out. The world around you starts to dissipate and as it slips away you open your mind's eye to find yourself in a meadow full of tall grasses. The grass is so long and you can barely see your way, but you are making your way towards some tall trees in the distance. You look up at the sun and notice that it has started to fall in the sky slightly, marking the start of the afternoon.

You are only part way across the meadow when you smell the faint scent of a bonfire. As you continue your journey you also hear the faint crackle and pop of burning wood. Then you step through the long grasses and into a clearing. In the centre of the clearing someone has set a bonfire.

You are wondering why there would be a fire here when a lady steps into the clearing carrying more wood for the fire. She tells you that the fire is almost ready for you. As you are wondering what on earth she is talking about, she continues by saying that before you can continue your journey into the woods you must first release your fears into the fire.

She indicates that you should walk through the flames whenever you are ready. For some reason you trust her and without fear you step into the flames. They don't feel hot at all but rather cleansing. They are burning away all that is holding you back. You are surrounded by flames dancing around you, flickering across your skin as you walk through the centre of the fire and out the other side.

The lady is there to greet you the other side and you realise that this is the goddess of July and the keeper of the flame. She gives you a special message and a small gift to remind you of your walk through the flames.

You thank her for the experience and the gift and continue on your journey towards the woodland feeling strengthened by the flames. As you step under the canopy of trees you become aware of your breath as it slowly moves in and out.

You slowly become aware of your surroundings again and give your fingers and toes a wiggle.

Take your time and open your eyes when you are ready, make a drink, eat some chocolate to ground and journal the message the goddess gave you.

Energy/Spell Work

This month should be full of sunshine (ever hopeful…) so work with the energy that the sun brings, it is also nearly the time of harvest to work towards the fruition of goals and projects. Don't forget to actually harvest…all the flowers, herbs and seeds from the garden, dry them and store for use at a later date. Work with the energies of this month for:

- Organisation
- Decisions
- Strength
- Emotions
- Will power
- Leadership

- Long term goals
- Planning
- Nurturing
- Perseverance
- Power
- Energy
- Happiness

Moon Lore

Our ancient ancestors tracked the passing of time by the phases of the moon. The full moon marking the start of the month, or moonth, and each lunation lasting approximately 29 days. Gradually each moon was given a name or a label, as we humans like to do. These names would be dictated by what was happening weather wise, like Thunder Moon or what activities were taking place – Hay Moon, for example. Unfortunately, there is no definitive list of names we can give, but throughout this course we will provide examples and more importantly we invite you to create your own list of names.

July's moon is often named Thunder Moon as the growing heat brings about storms that will hopefully alleviate the sweltering heat of the summer days. July also marks the start of the decline in the year. Now is the time to pause, bask in the warmth of the season or rest in the shade, while we stoke the inner fire that burns brightly in us all.

Names for the July Moon Include
Thunder Moon, Mead Moon, Blessing Moon, Corn Moon, Hay Moon

In the Celtic Tree Calendar
Oak Moon: 10th June-7th July; growth, success, blessings
Holly Moon: 8th July-4th August; celebration, wishes, protection

During this month's full moon go outside if you can and soak up her energies, let her speak to you and see what names come to you.

Ritual

We believe that personal rituals should be...well personal! So we have given you an outline guide for your own ritual, but it is up to you to invoke the deity/deities of your choice, relevant to this month would be good because that's the idea of this course, but if someone else is shouting 'pick me, pick me' don't ignore them. Add in your own individual ideas and style and make the ritual your own.

- Cast the circle
- Call in the quarters
- Invoke deity
- Smudge
- Work some magic or divination or just sit quietly and meditate
- Feast...
- Thank and dismiss the quarters
- Thank and bid farewell to deity
- Close the circle
- And don't forget to ground!

Crystals

Crystals have often been associated with each month and/or the magical energy that the month brings. Try popping one in your pocket, on your altar or meditate with one this month. Again go with your intuition but here are some to get you started:

- Ruby
- Carnelian
- Sunstone

- Amber
- Fire agate
- Pink tourmaline
- Rainbow moonstone
- Ruby
- Rhodonite
- Onyx
- Citrine
- Sardonyx
- Apache tears
- Peacock ore
- Chrysocolla
- Danburite
- Emerald
- Golden topaz
- Green tourmaline
- Kunzite
- Larimar
- Peridot
- Pink rhodochrosite
- Rutilated quartz
- Turquoise

Our Favourite Gem for July – Carnelian
This is a beautiful and powerful stone with so many uses. It carries the power of fertility and can assist in the relief of menopause and menstrual symptoms. Carnelian is an excellent stone to help relieve addictions of all kinds and helps with low self esteem.

Bury carnelians in the soil at sacred or ancient sites to help preserve and protect them (but do check with the owners of the site first to get permission).

A stone of abundance, carnelian works for personal wealth and the success of your business. It also helps with decision making.

Carnelian protects and can be placed around the home or carried on you. It brings strength, courage and helps you find your true self.

Use carnelian for past life work, love and sex magic and fire workings as well as for psychic protection.

Cleanse carnelians in sunlight or under running water. Keep carnelians in with your other stones to cleanse them from negative energy.

Crystal Grid

You could use the energies of this month to make a crystal grid. Start with a crystal in the centre and add your intent, if it is for business success you could put a business card under the centre crystal then add crystals going around in a spiral or a mandala pattern fanning out from the centre. I like to add herbs and oracle or tarot cards to my crystal grids too. Once your intuition has told you what crystals to use and where to put them, visualise all the crystals, herbs and cards linking up with a 'web' of white light to bring your intent to reality.

Oil/Incense Blends

Create an essential oil or a loose incense blend to use when you are meditating or just to help you work with the energies of this month. Here are some herbs and scents for incense that we associated with this month, but go with your own ideas:

- Lemon balm
- Sandalwood
- Myrrh
- Gardenia
- Bay
- Chamomile
- Saffron

- Rue
- Anise
- Burdock
- Camphor
- Dill
- Fennel
- Frankincense
- Heliotrope
- Galangal
- Lavender
- Lemon
- Marigold
- Mint
- Parsley
- Caraway
- Jasmine
- Mugwort
- Honeysuckle

Our Favourite Herb for July – Lemon Balm (Melissa officinalis)
This herb grows like a wild thing in my garden, I have had to confine it to pots otherwise it would take over! The bees absolutely love it even though the flowers are tiny, which makes it an excellent herb to use in bee magic and it self-seeds all over the place.

I think it looks a little bit like mint (probably because it is of the same family), but it has a beautiful lemon scent and flavour when you crush the leaves.

The Elizabethans apparently favoured lemon balm in food and drink not only for its taste, but also because it was said to relieve depression and aid in a good memory. I use it in sachets, medicine pouches and powders for both intents.

Lemon balm works really well in any success, healing or love workings. Carry lemon balm with you to ease anxiety and bring about balance and calm. Take a lemon balm leaf and wish for happiness upon it, leave the leaf to dry on your altar or beside your bed until it has worked its magic then burn the leaf and send a blessing of thanks.

And just in case…lemon balm is apparently very good for healing sword wounds…not that you get many of those nowadays, but it is always best to be prepared.

Essential Oil/Incense Recipe – Lazy Summer Days Incense
Mix together:

  2 parts frankincense
  2 parts sandalwood
  1 part bay
  A couple of drops of orange oil

Altar
We would love for you to create an altar for the month. Go with your heart, but think about what this month means to you, what the weather is like, what the magical energy represents and if a goddess came to you then a representation of her would be good too.

Stick with the summer sunshine theme for your altar and maybe add in some flowers and herbs from the garden and hedgerows.

Mandala
Mandala is a Sanskrit word meaning circle and is a spiritual and ritual symbol that represents the universe. A mandala will often have a square with four gates containing a circle with a centre point, but there are many variations.

Working with mandalas, whether you draw your own or colour in one that has already been created, can be a very relaxing and a surprisingly meditative exercise. You can find lots of free mandalas to download on the internet and colour, but also have a go at creating your own mandala for this month or for a particular goddess.

Pop on some quiet music, get your crayons out, release your inner child and allow yourself to be drawn into the mandala creation...you might be surprised what inspirations you find...

Once your mandala is finished, pop it on your altar.

Spirit Doll

Spirit dolls, poppets, goddess dolls...lots of different names from different cultures, but we thought it would be interesting to create a spirit doll, poppet or goddess representation for each month. Use whatever materials you have to hand or find easiest to work with – felt, cloth, string, Fimo, modelling clay...get creative.

Channel the energy of this month into your creation or add the characteristics and symbols of your chosen goddess.

If you make a doll from felt or material you can add herbs, spices and crystals to the inside too. If you work with clay or Fimo you can also incorporate herbs and crystals into the design.

The finished dolls will carry your very own magical energy with them together with the spirit of the month or the goddess you intended. Keep them on your altar.

Goddess Beauty

Calendula Cream

100g (3½oz) coconut oil
30g (1oz) calendula (marigold) petals

Other items needed:
2 Small saucepans
Clean jam jar

A cloth
Muslin cloth
Jar to store the finished cream in

Gently melt the coconut oil over a very low heat. Meanwhile, place the calendula petals in the jar. Once the coconut oil is melted, pour it into the jar, covering all the petals. Place the lid on loosely.

Then place your cloth in the bottom of the other saucepan and place the jar on the top. Fill with water until it covers the oil and petals in the jar.

Gently (don't let the water simmer) heat for 2 hours or longer if you want a really strong infusion and have the time. You probably don't want to leave it heating any longer than 6 hours though.

Once you have the strength of infusion required, strain the oil and petals through the muslin cloth and give it a really good squeeze to get every drop of liquid out. Then pour it into a jar and leave it to harden.

The cream is good for redness, sunburn, rashes and all sorts of ouchies. It is great for cracked and dry lips too.

Goddess Gift

The divine provides us with gifts...and we encourage you to step outside and see what the goddess, the divine, Mother Nature, has gifted you with.

It might be a feather, a pebble, a shell or maybe a leaf from a tree. Whatever you are gifted with you can add to your altar or maybe, if you are feeling artistic, you could create something with it.

A twig becomes a wand, a shell becomes a pendant, a feather becomes a smudge fan...think outside the box.

Medicine Bag

We have goddess medicine bags that we work with, just a square of material tied with a piece of thong, but inside we have representations of each goddess we have worked with. It helps us to keep a record of our journey, but also provides a focus for meditation and spiritual workings.

If you would like to create your own you can use a square of fabric. A bag made from felt or fabric works well too.

Each time you work with a different goddess ask them what symbol you should use to represent them in your medicine bag...you may be surprised.

By the end of this course you will have a wonderful collection of spiritual goddess items to keep in your own medicine bag.

Meditation Beads

Your mind can sometimes tend to wander when you are meditating, which leads to a loss of concentration. For practising meditation, meditation beads can act as a kind of 'anchor', or grounding point, enabling you to focus better. This can be extremely useful, especially if you are feeling tired when you meditate.

Conversely, if your mind is too active and over-energised, meditation beads will prevent you from becoming distracted or daydreaming. And, because the beads are moved in rhythm with your breathing, it helps you maintain your concentration.

At the end of this course you should have your own set of personal deities so you could create a string of meditation beads using one bead for each of your deities. It could be in the form of a necklace containing a bead for each of your twelve goddesses or you could make individual bracelets or pendants, one for each month.

The beads don't need to be used solely for meditation, you can use them throughout the day. When you awake, hold the beads and run them through your fingers and connect with their energy. This will set you up with positive intentions for the day.

Carry the beads with you in your pocket or bag, take them out during the day to remind you to stay grounded and focus on your tasks. Trust me, I need these all the time for focusing!

Hold the beads when you feel stressed or spacey to help bring you back centred and calm.

Finish your day the way you started by running the beads through your fingers and count your blessings. Release the negative points from your day and allow them to be replaced by the positive. Feel the good energy from the fabulous points of your day wash over you.

You also don't need to spend huge amounts of money. There are some beautiful meditation beads out there (often called prayer beads or malas), but you can make them yourself with whatever beads you have. There is no need to create a set of beads using expensive natural stones (although they are beautiful and full of natural energy). If all you have are wooden or plastic beads then use them, raid your children's play box even! The idea of the beads is to use them as a focus so even if you have a string of dried peas the intention is the same.

Feasting

We have included a recipe for each month – basically we don't need any excuse to include a cake recipe...but if you feel inclined to pop into the kitchen to bake we have given monthly suggestions on cakes to use in ritual to honour the goddess or just because they are yummy. If you love to cook you don't have to stop at cake, you could create a meal in honour of the goddess you are working with for the month (or just order a takeaway).

Cherry and Cinnamon Cake

> 200g (7oz) self raising flour
> 1 teaspoon ground cinnamon

75g (2½oz) caster sugar
2 eggs, beaten
6 tablespoons milk
100g (3½oz) butter, melted
350g (12oz) ripe cherries, de-stoned
Icing sugar for dusting

Preheat the oven to 180C/gas mark 4 and line and grease a cake tin.

Sift the flour into a bowl and add the cinnamon and caster sugar. Make a dip in the centre of the dry ingredients and add the egg, milk and melted butter. Beat everything together until you have a smooth and thick mixture. Spread the mix evenly in your tin.

Scatter the cherries over the mixture and gently press them in.

Bake in the oven for around 30-35 minutes until a skewer pushed into the centre comes out clean. Leave the cake to cool and, when it is cool enough to handle, take it out of the tin and leave it on a wire rack.

Dust the cake with icing sugar.

August

August brings the first of the harvests and is a time when the earth and her bounty start to give us the rewards followed by seeds to begin the cycle again.

The sun god enters his sage time, but is not yet done for...he loses his strength gradually each day as the nights grow longer.

We should not lament him, but instead celebrate the fruits of the harvest – not just the actual fruits and vegetables, but our own rewards for projects and goals we put into action earlier in the year.

Make the most of the last summer days and celebrate the bounty that Mother Earth provides for us.

Deities

In this part of the course we suggest nine goddesses that we associate with this month. Have a read through the information and see if any of them resonate with you. It may be that one of them comes to you in the meditation, it might be that another deity altogether greets you...go with your intuition. We have also included a list of some deities that have celebrations or feast days within this month too.

Arachne

Greek goddess of weaving and also believed to have been turned into a spider by Athena.

Arachne was a young woman who offended the goddess Athena by speaking the truth. Skilled in the art of weaving, Arachne studied under Athena and was challenged to produce a tapestry. Arachne embroidered a scene that showed the gods of Olympus in a bad light. Some stories say that, outraged, Athena turned Arachne into a spider, some say that Arachne was so sad that she killed herself and in a fit of remorse Athena changed her lifeless body into a spider.

Arachne is a goddess of time and of truth, she teaches her followers to speak the truth and to weave honesty within their lives from a place of love and concern instead of pride and ego.

Astarte
A Mesopotamian goddess of love and war, she is the power behind the moon. She is the all-encompassing power over the heavens and all of creation. She rules the spirit of the dead and is the mother of the astral bodies throughout the universe. She rules passion, marriage and sexual encounters, sensuality and the power of feminine independence. In her dark aspect she is the warrior queen, her passion channelled into victory and battle. Her symbols are the lion, the horse, the sphinx, the dove, and a star within a circle indicating the planet Venus. Pictorial representations often show her naked.

Ixchel
She is a Mayan goddess of the moon. As an ancient fertility goddess, Ix-Chel was responsible for sending rain to nourish the crops. When fulfilling that function she was called 'Lady Rainbow'. She helped ensure fertility by overturning her sacred womb jar so that the waters would flow. Though sometimes depicted as a goddess of catastrophe (the woman who stands by as the world floods), many of her myths show her in a more benevolent light—as a goddess who refused to become a victim of oppression. This was a woman who, when faced with adversity, took charge of her life and turned it around.

Medusa
Originating from Libya, she is a keeper of all feminine mysteries, she represents life and death, destroying to create anew. She also stands for the balance in nature and guards the entrance to earth, the heavens and the underworld. She is recognised by her hair

made from snakes that writhe upon her head.

The Norns

The Norns are three women who shape the life of each man from the day of his birth until his last dying breath, they also control when his last dying breath will be...the goddesses of fate.

The Norns reside in Asgard beside the Well of Urd, where the gods meet each day in council.

Urd is the eldest of the Norns and is old and decrepit, she focuses on the past.

Verdandi is the youngster, bright and attractive and looks straight before her.

Skuld is closely veiled and looks in the opposite direction to Urd.

The past, the present and the future.

Oshun

An ocean goddess from the Yoruban culture, she rules all bodies of water and is protector of women and witches. She embraces all that is sensual, fun and pleasurable. She loves dancing, perfume, sea shells and pretty jewellery.

Psyche

A Greek goddess and protector of the soul, love and happiness, she looks after all loving relationships and represents the transformation that a woman goes through from maiden to mother. She is often depicted with the wings of a bird or butterfly.

Heloise

She is a continental goddess who fell in love with a Breton scholar and used magic to keep their relationship together. Unfortunately they were both killed by the scholar's uncle and buried together in a tomb. The tale suggests that Heloise was a student druid. Work with her for love spells, druidry, sorcery and hand fasting rituals.

Minerva
A Roman goddess of wisdom, war, peace, knowledge, commerce and decisions. She is also a healing goddess and patron of healers. This clever gal is also an inventor, alchemist and a creator of numeracy and medicine.

Feast/Celebration Days
We have listed here the feast and celebration days for deities (we have included gods as well as goddesses) throughout August from various cultures and pantheons, these are taken from our own research...we apologise for any errors, but history is a fickle thing and calendars have changed over the years...

1ˢᵗ August
Lughnasadh/Lammas: Lughnasadh, also called Lammas, is the celebration of harvest. This is the time of the first harvests. At this celebration we give thanks to the earth for its bounty and beauty. It is from these harvests that we eat through the upcoming winter. The grain goddesses Demeter and Ceres are also honoured. This is a time to harvest the dreams planted earlier in the year. Lughnasadh, or Festival of Lugh, is a time of thanksgiving and reverence to the land for its sacrifices to us. The Lughnasadh Sabbat is a time to celebrate the first of three harvests. It marks the middle of summer and represents the start of the harvest cycle that relies on the early crops of ripening grain, and also any fruits and vegetables that are ready to be harvested. It is therefore greatly associated with bread as grain is one of the first crops to be harvested. Lughnasadh was also the traditional time of year for craft festivals. The medieval guilds would create elaborate displays of their wares, decorating their shops and themselves in bright colours and ribbons, marching in parades, and performing strange, ceremonial plays and dances

for entranced onlookers.

Blodeuwedd: In some parts of Britain it became customary to set a bonfire in a wagon wheel on a hilltop at Lushnasadh. When the wheel was glowing red it would be bowled down the hilltop as the community watched. It was to symbolise the descent of the sun from its midsummer height. This festival was also associated with the marriage of Lugh to Blodeuwedd.

Demeter and Ceres: The Roman festivals of late summer open the Mysteries of Life, a cycle that spans a quarter of the year. They celebrate the goddess as the source of all life, creatrix and sustainer of the cycles of existence through which the soul moves.

Macha: The annual fair of Macha was held at Armargh in Ireland to commemorate Queen Macha of the Golden Hair who had founded a palace there. The Three Machas were also associated with this feast.

New Year: Opening of the year and birthday of Egyptian sun god Ra-Horakhty.

3rd August

Guan Yin Enlightenment Day: Guan Yin is the Bodhisattva of Great Compassion in Mahayana Buddhism and is also worshipped by Taoists. The Bodhisattva was introduced into China via the Silk Road and, initially, Guan Yin was presented in male form. As Buddhism became localised in China, Guan Yin was subsequently transformed into Chinese female form. By the Song dynasty, Guan Yin evolved into a female bodhisattva in white robes that we see today. The male Guan Yin continues to be depicted, albeit less frequently. The bodhisattva's gender is unproblematic to devotees as Guan Yin will manifest in any form to reach out or to help suffering beings.

7th August

Karneia (Carneia): Festival in honour of Apollo held in the

Greek city of Sparta.

13th August

Hecate: The 13th of August marks a great festival for the Greek moon goddess Hecate and her descendant Diana. The goddess' aid is sought to avert storms, which might injure the coming harvest.

14th August-12th September

Hungry Ghosts Festival: The Chinese believe that on the seventh lunar month of each year, spirits of the deceased return to the human realm for a month. The seventh month is sometimes referred to as the ghost month and the festival is commonly known as the 'hungry ghost festival'. Many people avoid important events during the seventh month. Activities to avoid include moving to new homes, weddings, and opening ceremonies for new businesses.

15th August

Hapy and Amun: Offerings were made to Egyptian deities Hapy and Amun to secure a good flood.

Diana: The Festival of Torches was held on 15th August in honour of the Roman goddess Diana, where torches were hung in her groves.

19th August

Wag and Thoth: An Egyptian festival according to the great festival list in the temple for Ramesses III.

22nd August

Osiris: A great procession of the Egyptian god Osiris.

The Virgin Mary: The 22nd of August marks the Irish Octave of the Feast of the Assumption, the Immaculate Heart of the Blessed Virgin Mary, in the Christian list of festivals.

23rd August

Moira: This day is dedicated to the Greek Genia of Personal Fate. The threads of Moira draw all things in life together. Her symbols are the wheel and the scales. It is a day to examine the direction of your soul and make resolutions for the future.

Nemesis: The Greeks celebrated a festival called the Nemesia in memory of those departed, as the goddess Nemesis was supposed to defend the relics and memory of the dead from all insults.

25th August

Ops: Ops (meaning abundance) was the old Italian goddess of fertility, sowing and reaping and on the 25th of August she had a festival, the Opeconsiva, which only the Vestals and one of the pontifices could attend because her shrine in Regia was so tiny.

29th August

Hathor: Great festivals were held to celebrate the anniversary of the birth of the Egyptian goddess Hathor. Before dawn the priestesses would bring Hathor's image out onto the terrace to expose it to the rays of the rising sun. This was followed by much rejoicing, song and plenty of alcohol.

Teej: The Hindu festival of Teej is marked by fasting women who pray to Lord Shiva and goddess Parvati, seeking their blessings for marital bliss. It is a three-day festival that occurs on the third day of 'Shukla Paksha' or bright fortnight of the moon in the Hindu month of Shravana or Sawan, which falls during the Indian monsoon season, i.e., July to August. While ritual fasting is central to Teej, the festival is marked by colourful celebrations, especially by the women, who enjoy swing rides, song and dance. Swings are often hung from trees or placed in the courtyard of homes and decked with flowers. Young girls and married women apply mehendi or henna tattoos on this auspicious occasion. Women wear beautiful saris and adorn themselves with jewellery, and visit temples to offer their special prayers to goddess Parvati. A special sweet called 'ghewar' is prepared and distributed as Prasad or divine offering.

Manasa – the Snake Goddess: Ma Manasa Devi, the snake goddess, is worshipped by Hindus, mainly for the prevention and cure of snakebites and infectious diseases such as smallpox and chicken pox as well as for prosperity and fertility. She stands for both destruction and regeneration, almost akin to a snake shedding its skin and being reborn. The idol of the goddess is depicted as a graceful lady with her body adorned with snakes and sitting on a lotus or standing on a snake, under a hooded canopy of seven cobras. She is often seen as 'the one-eyed goddess', and sometimes portrayed with her son Astika on her lap. During the monsoon season, goddess Manasa is worshipped, mainly in the eastern Indian states of Bengal, Assam, Jharkand, and Orissa, throughout the months of June, July and August (Ashar – Shravan), a time when the snakes leave their nesting ground and come out into the open and become active. In Bangladesh, the Manasa and Ashtanaag Puja is a month-long affair spanning July and August. Devotees pay obeisance to goddess Manasa and perform various 'pujas' or rituals to appease her. Special 'murtis' or statues of the goddess are sculpted, sacrifices made and prayers chanted. In some places, worshippers are seen to pierce their bodies, poisonous snakes are displayed on the altar, and live shows depicting the life and legends of Manasa Devi are performed.

Raksha Bandhan Festival: The chaste bond of love between a brother and a sister is one of the deepest and noblest of human emotions. 'Raksha Bandhan' or 'Rakhi' is a special occasion to celebrate this emotional bonding by tying a holy thread around the wrist. This thread, which pulsates with sisterly love and sublime sentiments, is called the 'Rakhi'. It means 'a bond of protection', and Raksha Bandhan signifies that the strong must protect the weak from all that's evil. The ritual is observed on the full moon day of the Hindu month of Shravan, on which sisters tie the sacred Rakhi string on their brothers' right wrists, and pray for their long life. Rakhis are ideally made of silk with gold and silver threads, beautifully crafted embroidered sequins and studded with semi precious stones. This ritual not only strengthens the bond of love between brothers and sisters, but also transcends the confines of the family. When a Rakhi is tied on the wrists of close friends and neighbours, it underscores the need for a harmonious social life, where every individual co-exist peacefully as brothers and sisters. All members of the community commit to protect each other and the society

Mid August

Pamboeotia: Dedicated to Zeus Panemeros and Athena.

Meditation

Take a deep breath in through your nose and a long sigh out through your mouth. Feel any tension in your body start to melt away as you become comfortable and relaxed. Take another breath in through your nose, the air going deep into your stomach, then slowly and gently release the breath out through your mouth.

Your everyday thoughts and worries fade away as you bring your attention solely to your breath as it moves gently in and slowly out. The world around you starts to dissipate and as it slips away you open your mind's eye to find yourself at the edge of woodland. It is a warm sunny day and the shade of the trees looks so inviting, but there is a large stretch of water between you and the comfort of their shade. The water is far too wide to jump across and looks quite deep too. You are disappointed thinking there is no way to cross and you turn trying to find another path when a woman calls to you. 'There is always a way if you know where to look,' she says.

You look back at the apparently impassable river, but still can't see a way.

'Look with your inner eyes,' the woman says.

You soften your gaze and as soon as you do you see a bridge appear leading right over the water.

You turned to her, stunned. She smiles a knowing smile. Then she gives you a message just for you. When she is finished, she hands you a little gift and tells you that she is the matriarch and the goddess of August. You thank her for her guidance and gift and make your way over the bridge.

Once across the bridge you step onto the opposite bank and turn to wave at the matriarch, but she has already gone. You step under the canopy of trees and as you feel the coolness of their shade you start to become aware of your breath as it slowly moves in and out.

You slowly become aware of your surroundings again and give your fingers and toes a wiggle.

Take your time and open your eyes when you are ready, make a drink, eat some chocolate (or other food if you can't eat chocolate) to ground and then journal any messages the goddess gave you.

Energy/Spell Work

Work with the energies of the harvest, abundance and reaping what you have sown. Magical workings for August could include:

- Connectedness
- Career
- Health
- Financial gain
- Abundance
- Grounding
- Cleansing
- Decisions
- Purification

Moon Lore

Our ancient ancestors tracked the passing of time by the phases of the moon. The full moon marking the start of the month, or moonth, and each lunation lasting approximately 29 days. Gradually each moon was given a name or a label, as we humans like to do. These names would be dictated by what was happening seasonally, like Dog Days Moon, or what activities were taking place – Harvest Moon or Hunting Moon, for example. Unfortunately, there is no definitive list of names we can give, but throughout this course we will provide examples and more importantly we invite you to create your own list of names.

August's moon is named after the harvest and association grains that are ripe and ready to be brought in. Use the moon's vibrant energy this month and channel it into reaping your own personal harvest.

Names for the August Moon Include
Harvest Moon, Corn Moon, Grain Moon, Herb Moon, Dog Days Moon

In the Celtic Tree Calendar
Holly Moon: 8th July-4th August; celebration, wishes, protection
Hazel Moon: 5th August-1st September; inner wisdom, intuition

During this month's full moon go outside if you can and soak up her energies, let her speak to you and see what names come to you.

Ritual

We believe that personal rituals should be…well personal! So we have given you an outline guide for your own ritual, but it is up to you to invoke the deity/deities of your choice, relevant to this month would be good because that's the idea of this course, but if someone else is shouting 'pick me, pick me' don't ignore them. Add in your own individual ideas and style and make the ritual your own.

- Cast the circle
- Call in the quarters
- Invoke deity
- Smudge
- Work some magic or divination or just sit quietly and meditate
- Feast...
- Thank and dismiss the quarters
- Thank and bid farewell to deity
- Close the circle
- And don't forget to ground!

Crystals
Crystals have often been associated with each month and/or the magical energy that the month brings. Try popping one in your pocket, on your altar or meditate with one this month. Again go with your intuition, but here are some to get you started:

- Peridot
- Bronzite
- Aventurine
- Citrine
- Sardonyx
- Cat's eye
- Golden topaz
- Obsidian
- Moss agate
- Rhodochrosite
- Quartz
- Marble

- Granite
- Lodestone
- Carnelian
- Amber
- Sunstones
- Pink tourmaline
- Garnet
- Amazonite
- Sapphire
- Blue topaz

Our Favourite Gem for August – Peridot

Peridot is a total money stone, bringing wad loads of cash your way along with a side order of luck and maybe a lil' bit of love too...

This pretty pale green stone is also an excellent all-round healer on a physical level, particularly bringing cooling and soothing energy for fevers, swelling, asthma and allergic reactions, but it also brings peace and calm to your spirit and soul.

Pop a peridot stone into your purse, a medicine pouch or just inside your front door to bring money in.

Peridot brings good luck to your marriage and can also be used as a stone to dispel negative energy and send it back to the source.

Crystal Grid

You could use the energies of this month to make a crystal grid. Start with a crystal in the centre and add your intent, if it is for business success you could put a business card under the centre crystal then add crystals going around in a spiral or a mandala pattern fanning out from the centre. I like to add herbs and oracle or tarot cards to my crystal grids too. Once your intuition has told you what crystals to use and where to put them, visualise all the crystals, herbs and cards linking up with a 'web' of white light to bring your intent to reality.

Oil/Incense Blends

Create an essential oil or a loose incense blend to use when you are meditating or just to help you work with the energies of this month. Here are some herbs and scents for incense that we associated with this month, but go with your own ideas:

- Heather
- Blackberry
- Sloe
- Crab apple
- Pear
- Goldenrod
- Peony
- Nasturtium
- Clover
- Yarrow
- Heliotrope
- Vervain
- Rose
- Sunflower
- Poppy
- Grains (wheat, corn, rye, oat, barley)
- Garlic
- Basil
- Mint
- Meadowsweet
- Apple
- Raspberry
- Strawberry
- Mugwort
- Hops

- Marigold
- Ivy
- Elder
- Hazelnut
- Rosemary
- Frankincense

Our Favourite Herb for August – Meadowsweet (Spiraea filipendula, Filipendula ulmaria, Spirea ulmaria)
An herb that smells of freshly mown grass, it reminds me of summer and skipping through daisy filled meadows (okay I don't actually get to do that much, but the thought is there). It has a really happy, blissful and peaceful energy.

My research guides me to the suggestion that the name 'meadow' is more to do with the drink mead than grassy meadows (which is always a good thing), the flowers of meadowsweet having been used for centuries to flavour mead, wine and beer.

Keep meadowsweet in the house to ensure a happy and peaceful home.

Use it in love, peace and happiness spell work.

(Caution: if you are allergic to aspirin you may find the same with meadowsweet).

Essential Oil/Incense Recipe – Guardians of the Forest Incense
Mix together:

3 parts pine needles
1 part thyme
A couple of drops patchouli oil

Altar
We would love for you to create an altar for the month. Go with your heart, but think about what this month means to you, what

the weather is like, what the magical energy represents and if a goddess came to you then a representation of her would be good too.

Go mad with the harvest fruits and vegetable theme...

Mandala

Mandala is a Sanskrit word meaning circle and is a spiritual and ritual symbol that represents the universe. A mandala will often have a square with four gates containing a circle with a centre point, but there are many variations.

Working with mandalas, whether you draw your own or colour in one that has already been created, can be a very relaxing and a surprisingly meditative exercise. You can find lots of free mandalas to download on the internet and colour, but also have a go at creating your own mandala for this month or for a particular goddess.

Pop on some quiet music, get your crayons out, release your inner child and allow yourself to be drawn into the mandala creation...you might be surprised what inspirations you find...

Once your mandala is finished, pop it on your altar.

Spirit Doll

Spirit dolls, poppets, goddess dolls...lots of different names from different cultures, but we thought it would be interesting to create a spirit doll, poppet or goddess representation for each month. Use whatever materials you have to hand or find easiest to work with – felt, cloth, string, Fimo, modelling clay...get creative.

Channel the energy of this month into your creation or add the characteristics and symbols of your chosen goddess.

If you make a doll from felt or material you can add herbs, spices and crystals to the inside too. If you work with clay or Fimo you can also incorporate herbs and crystals into the design.

The finished dolls will carry your very own magical energy

with them together with the spirit of the month or the goddess you intended. Keep them on your altar.

Goddess Beauty

Blueberry Summer Facial

> 25g (1oz) blueberries
> 1 tablespoon honey
> 1 tablespoon olive oil

Put all three ingredients in your blender until they reach a rich creamy consistency. Apply it all over your face, avoiding your eyes, and let the antioxidants seep in. Rinse and pat your face dry. You should be left with a soft and beautiful summer glow.

Goddess Gift

The divine provides us with gifts...and we encourage you to step outside and see what the goddess, the divine, Mother Nature, has gifted you with.

It might be a feather, a pebble, a shell or maybe a leaf from a tree. Whatever you are gifted with you can add to your altar or maybe, if you are feeling artistic, you could create something with it.

A twig becomes a wand, a shell becomes a pendant, a feather becomes a smudge fan...think outside the box.

Medicine Bag

We have goddess medicine bags that we work with, just a square of material tied with a piece of thong, but inside we have representations of each goddess we have worked with. It helps us to keep a record of our journey, but also provides a focus for meditation and spiritual workings.

If you would like to create your own you can use a square of fabric. A bag made from felt or fabric works well too.

Each time you work with a different goddess ask them what symbol you should use to represent them in your medicine bag...you may be surprised.

By the end of this course you will have a wonderful collection of spiritual goddess items to keep in your own medicine bag.

Meditation Beads

Your mind can sometimes tend to wander when you are meditating, which leads to a loss of concentration. For practising meditation, meditation beads can act as a kind of 'anchor', or grounding point, enabling you to focus better. This can be extremely useful, especially if you are feeling tired when you meditate.

Conversely, if your mind is too active and over-energised, meditation beads will prevent you from becoming distracted or daydreaming. And, because the beads are moved in rhythm with your breathing, it helps you maintain your concentration.

At the end of this course you should have your own set of personal deities so you could create a string of meditation beads using one bead for each of your deities. It could be in the form of a necklace containing a bead for each of your twelve goddesses or you could make individual bracelets or pendants, one for each month.

The beads don't need to be used solely for meditation, you can use them throughout the day. When you awake, hold the beads and run them through your fingers and connect with their energy. This will set you up with positive intentions for the day.

Carry the beads with you in your pocket or bag, take them out during the day to remind you to stay grounded and focus on your tasks. Trust me, I need these all the time for focusing!

Hold the beads when you feel stressed or spacey to help bring you back centred and calm.

Finish your day the way you started by running the beads

through your fingers and count your blessings. Release the negative points from your day and allow them to be replaced by the positive. Feel the good energy from the fabulous points of your day wash over you.

You also don't need to spend huge amounts of money. There are some beautiful meditation beads out there (often called prayer beads or malas), but you can make them yourself with whatever beads you have. There is no need to create a set of beads using expensive natural stones (although they are beautiful and full of natural energy). If all you have are wooden or plastic beads then use them, raid your children's play box even! The idea of the beads is to use them as a focus so even if you have a string of dried peas the intention is the same.

Feasting

We have included a recipe for each month – basically we don't need any excuse to include a cake recipe…but if you feel inclined to pop into the kitchen to bake we have given monthly suggestions on cakes to use in ritual to honour the goddess or just because they are yummy. If you love to cook you don't have to stop at cake, you could create a meal in honour of the goddess you are working with for the month (or just order a takeaway).

White Chocolate Chip Scones

There can't be anything more summery than a plate of homemade scones dripping with jam and cream. Here I have included two different fillings – sliced fresh strawberries and caramel fudge.

225g (8oz) self raising flour
1 teaspoon baking powder
50g (2oz) butter or margarine
25g (1oz) sugar
1 tablespoon white chocolate chips

7 tablespoons milk

Pre heat the oven to 220C/425F/Gas Mark 7.

Grease a baking sheet.

Place all the ingredients together in a bowl and mix to form a soft dough. I do this in the food mixer with a paddle fitted.

Turn it onto a lightly floured board, knead slightly to smooth then roll out to a thickness of about ½ inch. The thicker your uncooked scones are the higher they will be when they cook, so if you like sky scraper scones roll them out to about ¾ inch. Don't roll them flatter than ½ inch otherwise you will end up with flat scones.

Cut them into rounds with a floured cookie cutter.

Place these on the baking sheet and brush the tops with some extra milk.

Bake them in the pre-heated oven for 12-15 minutes until they have risen and are golden brown.

You can ring the changes by adding dark or milk chocolate chips or dried sultanas or dried cranberries...be creative.

Fillings
Whisk up a tub of double (heavy) cream with a tablespoon of sugar and ½ teaspoon vanilla extract until it forms soft peaks.

The scones can be split in half and either spread with jam and layered with the cream and sliced strawberries or you can add caramel spread and crumbled fudge. Either way they are deliciously messy and sweet.

September

September is the month for the second harvest, the autumn equinox (or Mabon, although that is a more modern term).

The leaves are starting to turn towards their autumn hue and the farmers are working in the fields to bring us the produce. The sun is still shining, the days are often still warm, but the mornings and evenings bring that autumnal chill.

The equinox is the balance of light and dark; from now on the days become increasingly shorter.

September is a month to celebrate and be thankful for what we have, our own personal harvest. It is also a good time to take stock and check that the plans we put into motion earlier in the year are all working as we had hoped.

The god sacrifices himself at the autumn equinox; sometimes sacrifice is necessary to allow us to move forward...

Deities

In this part of the course we suggest nine goddesses that we associate with this month. Have a read through the information and see if any of them resonate with you. It may be that one of them comes to you in the meditation, it might be that another deity altogether greets you...go with your intuition. We have also included a list of some deities that have celebrations or feast days within this month too.

Artemis

Twin sister of Apollo, Artemis is the Greek goddess of wild animals, the wilderness in general, the hunt, and a protectress of womankind in all its aspects. Ruler of the nymphs (who are notorious for their sexual dalliance), she remains a symbol of chastity and indifference to men. She is a patroness of childbirth, in the role of nurse and midwife. Her temper is legendary, but her images invariable display her in a calm and beneficent mood. She is the protector of young girls until they reach the age of marriage.

As the virgin huntress she is independent, self reliant and a defender of the weak and abused.

Her symbols are the deer, the bear, the bow and the cypress tree.

Diana

Roman goddess of witches, the moon, patroness of groves, forests and the natural world. She is a huntress and protector of animals. She is known for her great beauty, magical skills and protection of witches. She also has authority over childbirth and midwifery.

Druantia

This Celtic goddess is said to be queen of the druids; she brings wisdom and knowledge and is protector of all trees. Seek her out to find guidance to your true path, passion, fertility and the ancient knowledge of the dryads.

Asherah

Queen of the gods and ruler of heaven from the Middle East, she is a curly haired goddess that rides a sacred lion. She is the consort to Yahweh and a goddess of the sea, divine wisdom and femininity. Her symbols are the tree of life, lilies and cows.

Spider Woman

A Native American creatrix goddess, she is the great teacher, the creator of life and weaver of dreams. She uses her power to weave all time and to bind reality to the unknown.

Ratis

An ancient British goddess connected with the hill forts of Northumberland, she is a strong and powerful goddess to call upon for protection.

Proserpina
Roman maiden goddess of spring, she rules over agriculture and all that grows and blooms. In her dark maiden aspect she rules the underworld with Pluto.

Jord
Norse giantess goddess of the earth and all the wild lands, she is a giver of life. She is the mother of Thor and the mistress of Odin.

Aja
Goddess of forests from West African, she is a healer and wise woman ruling over forests, woods and all herbal medicine, teaching her skills to those that seek them.

Feast/Celebration Days
We have listed here the feast and celebration days for deities (we have included gods as well as goddesses) throughout September from various cultures and pantheons. These are taken from our own research...we apologise for any errors but history is a fickle thing and calendars have changed over the years...

4th-19th September
Ludi Romani/Ludi Magni: 'Roman Games' or 'Great Games'. The Ludi Romani were held in honour of Jupiter Optimus Maximus. They were originally held only on 13th September, but were gradually expanded until they were held over sixteen days by the time of the Empire. The Ludi Romani began with a solemn procession from Jupiter's temple on the Capitoline to the Circus Maximus. Sacrifices were made to Jupiter, and circus performances were given.

5th September
Genesia: Greek festival in honour of the dead.

8th September
Virgin Mary: The birth of the Virgin Mary is celebrated by Christians.

12th September
Birthday of Ksitigarbha Bodhisattva: The Bodhisattva of Great Aspiration is one of the most well-known Bodhisattvas in Chinese Mahayana Buddhism. He is also known as Di Zhang Wang Pusa in Chinese and commonly translated as Earth Store Bodhisattva. The Bodhisattva is also commonly worshipped in Taoist temples, especially at the ancestral halls. The Bodhisattva is known for his great vow to help beings in all realms to gain enlightenment before he would become a Buddha. He is also tasked to teach the Dharma to all beings during the time between the passing of the historical Buddha (Gautama Buddha) and the arrival of Maitreya Buddha.

Mid Autumn Festival: On the 15th day of the 8th lunar month, the Chinese celebrate the Mid Autumn Festival, also known as the Moon Festival and Lantern Festival. Since the mid autumn follows the lunar calendar, the dates change every year. This day is also the birthday of Old Man Under the Moon, the matchmaker.

13th September
Epulum Iovis: 'Feast of Jupiter'. This feast was attended by Roman senators and high ranking magistrates during the Ludi Romani and Ludi Plebeii. It started with the sacrifice of a white cow and ritual cakes to honour Jupiter, and possibly Juno and Minerva.
Lectisternia: This festival was held to honour the Capitoline

Triad: Jupiter, Juno, and Minerva.

13th/15th September-21st/22nd September

Eleusinian Mysteries: This ancient Greek festival was held by those of the Eleusinian religion based on the myth of Demeter and Kore (Persephone).

15th September

Amun: Start of Ipet festival which ran for eleven days in honour of Amun in Luxor, Egypt.

16th/17th September

Vishwakarma Puja: Vishwakarma is the presiding deity of all craftsmen and architects. Son of Brahma, he is the divine draftsman of the whole universe, and the official builder of all the gods' palaces. Vishwakarma is also the designer of all the flying chariots of the gods, and all their weapons. Hindus widely regard Vishwakarma as the god of architecture and engineering, and 16th or 17th September every year is celebrated as Vishwakarma Puja — a resolution time for workers and craftsmen to increase productivity and gain divine inspiration for creating novel products. This ritual usually takes place within the factory premises or shop floor, and the otherwise mundane workshops come alive with fiesta. Vishwakarma Puja is also associated with the buoyant custom of flying kites. This occasion in a way also marks the start of the festive season that culminates in Diwali.

18th September

Khnum and Anuqet: Local Elephantine festival of Egyptian deities Khnum and Anuqet.

21st/22nd/23rd September

The Autumn Equinox: Two days a year, the northern and

southern hemispheres receive the same amount of sunlight. Not only that, each receives the same amount of light as they do dark. In Latin, the word equinox translates to 'equal night'. The autumn equinox takes place on or near 21st September, and its spring counterpart falls around 21st March. If you're in the northern hemisphere, the days will begin getting shorter after the autumn equinox and the nights will grow longer, in the southern hemisphere, the reverse is true. The harvest is a time of thanks, and also a time of balance. While we celebrate the gifts of the earth, we also accept that the soil is dying. We have food to eat, but the crops are brown and going dormant. Warmth is behind us, cold lies ahead. For contemporary druids, this is the celebration of Alban Elfed, which is a time of balance between the light and the dark. Many Asatru groups honour this equinox as Winter Nights, a festival sacred to Freyr.

Demeter and Persephone: Perhaps the best known of all the harvest mythologies is the story of Demeter and Persephone. Demeter was a goddess of grain and of the harvest in ancient Greece. Her daughter, Persephone, caught the eye of Hades, god of the underworld. When Hades abducted Persephone and took her back to the underworld, Demeter's grief caused the crops on earth to die and go dormant. By the time she finally recovered her daughter, Persephone had eaten six pomegranate seeds, and so was doomed to spend six months of the year in the underworld. These six months are the time when the earth dies, beginning at the time of the autumn equinox.

Inanna: The Sumerian goddess Inanna is the incarnation of fertility and abundance. Inanna descended into the underworld where her sister, Ereshkigal, ruled. Ereshkigal decreed that Inanna could only enter her world in the traditional ways stripping herself of her clothing and earthly possessions. By the time Inanna got there, Ereshkigal had unleashed a series of plagues upon her sister, killing Inanna. While Inanna was visiting the underworld, the earth ceased to grow and produce. A vizier restored Inanna to life, and sent her back to earth. As she journeyed home, the earth was restored to its former glory.

28th September

Birthday of the Monkey God: The Monkey God is one of the most popular characters in Chinese culture and is worshipped as a Taoist deity. The Monkey God was born from a rock left behind from goddess Nuwa's creation of the universe. After being conditioned by natural forces, the Monkey God emerged from this piece of rock.

Satet and Anuqet: Local Elephantine festival of Satet and Anuqet in Egypt.

30th September

Meditrinalia: During this Roman festival fruits were offered to Meditrina as a goddess of medicine.

Mahalakshmi or Varalakshmi Vrata: This is a special vrata or fast dedicated to Hindu goddess 'Mahalakshmi,' or as the name implies 'Great Lakshmi' (maha = great). Lakshmi is the presiding deity of wealth, prosperity, light, wisdom, fortune, fertility, generosity and courage. These eight facets of Lakshmi give rise to another name for the goddess — 'Ashtalakshmi' (ashta = eight). According to the lunar calendar of North India, the Mahalakshmi Vrata fast is observed for 16 days in a row between Bhadrapad Shukla Ashtami and Ashwin Krishna Ashtami, i.e., commencing on the 8th day of the bright fortnight of the month of Bhadra and ending on the 8th day of the dark fortnight of the following month Ashwin, which corresponds to September to October of the international calendar. The fast is more popular in Uttar Pradesh Bihar, Jharkhand and Madhya Pradesh than other states of India. At the dawn of this holy day, women take a ritual bath and pray to Surya, the sun god. They sprinkle sacred water using purified grass blades or 'durva' on their body and tie sixteen knotted strings on their left wrist. A pot or 'kalasha' is filled with water, decorated with betel or mango leaves, and a coconut is placed on top of it. It is further adorned with a red cotton cloth or 'shalu' and a red thread is tied around it. A Swastika symbol and four lines, representing the four Vedas are drawn on it with vermillion or 'sindoor/kumkum'. Also called the Purna Kumbh, this represents the supreme deity and is worshipped as the goddess Mahalakshmi. Holy lamps are lit, incense sticks are burned and Lakshmi mantras are chanted during the 'puja' or ritual worship.

Ganesha Chaturthi: The great Ganesha festival, also known as 'Vinayak Chaturthi' or 'Vinayaka Chavithi', is celebrated by Hindus around the world as the birthday of Lord Ganesha. It is observed during the Hindu month of Bhadra (mid-August to mid-September) and the grandest and most elaborate of them, especially in the western India state of Maharashtra, lasts for ten days, ending on the day of 'Ananta Chaturdashi'. A life-like clay model of Lord Ganesha is made two to three months prior to the day of Ganesh Chaturthi. The size of this idol may vary from less than an inch to more than 25 feet. On the day of the festival, it is placed on raised platforms in homes or in elaborately decorated outdoor tents for people to view and pay their homage. The priest, usually clad in red silk dhoti and shawl, then invokes life into the idol amid the chanting of mantras. This ritual is called 'pranapratishhtha'. After this the 'shhodashopachara' (sixteen ways of paying tribute) follows. Coconut, jaggery, 21 'modakas' (rice flour preparation), 21 'durva' (trefoil) blades and red flowers are offered. The idol is anointed with red unguent or sandal paste (rakta chandan). Throughout the ceremony, Vedic hymns from the Rig Veda and Ganapati Atharva Shirsha Upanishad, and Ganesha stotra from the Narada Purana are chanted.

For ten days, from Bhadrapad Shudh Chaturthi to the Ananta Chaturdashi, Ganesha is worshipped. On the 11th day, the image is taken through the streets in a procession accompanied with dancing and singing, to be immersed in a river or the sea symbolising a ritual see-off of the Lord in his journey towards his abode in Kailash while taking away with him the misfortunes of all men.

All join in this final procession shouting 'Ganapathi Bappa Morya, Purchya Varshi Laukariya' (O father Ganesha, come again early next year). After the final offering of coconuts, flowers and camphor is made, then people carry the idol to the river to immerse it.

Pitri-Paksha: The annual ancestor-worship or 'Pitri-Paksha' is a period that is observed during the dark half of the Hindu month of 'Ashwin'. This period of 15 days is set aside by the Hindus for the remembrance of their ancestors. During this fortnight, Hindus donate food to the hungry in the hope that their ancestors will also be fed. It is this time that Hindus throughout the world reflect on the contributions their forefathers made to their present life, and the cultural norms, traditions and values they set for us in order to make our lives better. (Dates vary each year during September/October).

Durga Puja: The ceremonial worship of the mother goddess is one of the most important festivals of India. Apart from being a religious festival for the Hindus, it is also an occasion for reunion and rejuvenation, and a celebration of traditional culture and customs. While the rituals entails ten days of fast, feast and worship, the last four days – Saptami, Ashtami, Navami and Dashami – are celebrated with much gaiety and grandeur in India and abroad, especially in Bengal, where the ten-armed goddess, Durga Puja, is celebrated every year in the Hindu month of Ashwin (September-October). It commemorates Prince Rama's invocation of the goddess before going to war with the demon king Ravana. This autumnal ritual was different from the conventional Durga Puja, which is usually celebrated in the springtime. So, this Puja is also known as 'akal-bodhan' or out-of-season ('akal') worship ('bodhan'). Thus goes the story of Lord Rama, who first worshipped the 'Mahishasura Mardini' or the slayer of the buffalo-demon, by offering 108 blue lotuses and lighting 108 lamps, at this time of the year.

Proerosia: A festival that involved praying to Demeter for a good harvest before Ancient Greeks began ploughing and sowing.

Meditation

Take a deep breath in through your nose and a long sigh out through your mouth. Feel any tension in your body start to melt away as you become comfortable and relaxed. Take another breath in through your nose, the air going deep into your stomach, then slowly and gently release the breath out through your mouth.

Your everyday thoughts and worries fade away as you bring your attention solely to your breath as it moves gently in and slowly out. The world around you starts to dissipate and as it slips away you open your mind's eye to find yourself at the edge of a forest. It is late afternoon and the sun is starting to set, so you turn your attention back to the forest where a young deer has just come out from beneath the trees.

You step into the forest and under the canopy of the trees it seems even darker. You can hear the sounds of birds as they start preparing the roost for the night. Gentle scurrying sounds are coming from the under-growth where animals are getting ready for their evening. You look up at the trees above you and notice the leaves have started to change colour. Bright yellows, reds and gold surround you in the shelter above.

You think about the transformation the leaves are going through and compare it to the transformation you have gone through in your life and wonder what this journey today will bring.

From out of the trees steps a woman with a gown made of autumn leaves and a cloak of green moss. She is a reflection of the forest itself. She invites you to walk a way through the forest with her and as you do she shares a message that is just for you.

As you are walking through the forest you notice animals of all shapes and sizes are also walking with you, or rather with this captivating autumn goddess. She is the guardian of the forest and the protector of all woodland creatures.

She brings you to a stop at the edge of the lake and tells you that this is where she must leave you. She gives you a gift as a reminder of your journey through the forest. Then you are standing at the edge of the lake on your own. You look into the lake and your reflection looks back at you, showing you the transformations you have undertaken and those yet to come. Once the images have stopped you start to become aware of breath as it slowly moves in and out.

You slowly become aware of your surroundings again and give your fingers and toes a wiggle.

Take your time and open your eyes when you are ready, make a drink, eat some chocolate (or other food if you cannot eat chocolate) to ground. Journal any messages the goddess gave you.

Energy/Spell Work

Work with the energies of the equinox; give thanks to the waning sunlight and for the abundance of the crops. Honour the gods of nature and celebrate the goddess as she passes from the stage of mother to that of crone and the god as he prepares for death and re-birth. Finish projects that are hanging about, tidy up, sort and prepare for the coming part of the year where we rest, relax and reflect. Work with the energies of this month for:

- Protection
- Balance
- Prosperity
- Security
- Self confidence
- Harmony
- Balance

- Fertility
- Independence
- Feminine issues
- Love
- Relationships
- Sex magic
- Health
- Psychic abilities

Moon Lore

Our ancient ancestors tracked the passing of time by the phases of the moon. The full moon marking the start of the month, or moonth, and each lunation lasting approximately 29 days. Gradually each moon was given a name or a label, as we humans like to do. These names would be dictated by what was happening seasonally, like Fruit Moon, or what activities were taking place – Harvest Moon or Hunting Moon, for example. Unfortunately, there is no definitive list of names we can give, but throughout this course we will provide examples and more importantly we invite you to create your own list of names.

September's moon is another harvest moon, but this time it is fruits instead of grains. So we find this moon named after the vine or blackberries. September also is the time of the equinox when the days and nights stand equally in balance. We can now start to make plans and preparations for the approaching autumn.

Names for the September's Moon Include
Vine Moon, Harvest Moon, Blackberry Moon, Fruit Moon, Barley Moon

In the Celtic Tree Calendar
Hazel Moon: 5th August-1st September; inner wisdom, intuition
Vine Moon: 2nd September-30th September; balance, bringing

plans to fruition

During this month's full moon go outside if you can and soak up her energies, let her speak to you and see what names come to you.

Ritual

We believe that personal rituals should be...well personal! So we have given you an outline guide for your own ritual, but it is up to you to invoke the deity/deities of your choice, relevant to this month would be good because that's the idea of this course, but if someone else is shouting 'pick me, pick me' don't ignore them. Add in your own individual ideas and style and make the ritual your own.

- Cast the circle
- Call in the quarters
- Invoke deity
- Smudge
- Work some magic or divination or just sit quietly and meditate
- Feast...
- Thank and dismiss the quarters
- Thank and bid farewell to deity
- Close the circle
- And don't forget to ground!

Crystals

Crystals have often been associated with each month and/or the magical energy that the month brings. Try popping one in your pocket, on your altar or meditate with one this month. Again go with your intuition but here are some to get you started:

- Sapphire

- Bloodstone
- Rainbow obsidian
- Lapis lazuli
- Agate
- Topaz
- Carnelian
- Amethyst
- Hag stones (river or ocean stones with holes through)
- Moss agate
- Peridot
- Amazonite
- Amber
- Blue topaz
- Chrysocolla
- Dioptase
- Green tourmaline
- Lodestone
- Sodalite
- Suglite
- Aquamarine
- Sunstone

Our Favourite Gem for September – Lapis Lazuli
This is a stone often associated with the gods and the divine. It is associated with the brow chakra. It also helps relieve headaches and anxiety.

Keep lapis in the home to bring loyalty and contentment and in the office to help with trust issues and promotion prospects.

Keep lapis under your pillow to help give a peaceful night's sleep.

Use it for psychic protection, prophetic dreams and in all night magic workings.

Recharge your lapis stones under the moonlight.

Crystal Grid
You could use the energies of this month to make a crystal grid. Start with a crystal in the centre and add your intent, if it is for business success you could put a business card under the centre crystal then add crystals going around in a spiral or a mandala pattern fanning out from the centre. I like to add herbs and oracle or tarot cards to my crystal grids too. Once your intuition has told you what crystals to use and where to put them, visualise all the crystals, herbs and cards linking up with a 'web' of white light to bring your intent to reality.

Oil/Incense Blends
Create an essential oil or a loose incense blend to use when you are meditating or just to help you work with the energies of this month. Here are some herbs and scents for incense that we associated with this month, but go with your own ideas:

- Acorn
- Benzoin
- Fern
- Grains
- Honeysuckle
- Marigold
- Milkweed
- Myrrh
- Passionflower
- Rose
- Sage
- Solomon's Seal
- Thistle
- Patchouli
- Cinnamon
- Pine
- Apple

- Frankincense
- Sandalwood
- Cypress
- Juniper
- Oak
- Marjoram
- Thyme

Our Favourite Herb for September – Patchouli (Pogostemon)
Although a plant native to tropical climates and not one I can grow in my own garden, I have included it because it is one of my favourites... If you can't get hold of the dried herb itself you can use patchouli oil or I have even used crushed up patchouli incense sticks on occasion.

Patchouli is a bushy herb from the mint family with tall stems that have pale pink/white flowers. Patchouli has a strong earthy scent that has been used for centuries in perfume and medicine.

It is an excellent herb for grounding and earth magic and connecting with Mother Earth and her elementals. Patchouli can be used in all kinds of prosperity and money spells. It also works very well in protective magic workings.

Patchouli is said to be an aphrodisiac, so this herbs works incredibly well in sex magic spells...be warned...it's pretty potent...

Burn it in incense blends to bring balance, peace and calm.

Essential Oil/Incense Recipe – Ladies of the Lake Oil
Mix together:

2 drops sandalwood
2 drops lavender
3 drops rose (substitute palma rose as it is much cheaper)

Altar

We would love for you to create an altar for the month. Go with your heart, but think about what this month means to you, what the weather is like, what the magical energy represents and if a goddess came to you then a representation of her would be good too.

Go all out with leaves and natural items that show signs of autumn, maybe even a gourd or two.

Mandala

Mandala is a Sanskrit word meaning circle and is a spiritual and ritual symbol that represents the universe. A mandala will often have a square with four gates containing a circle with a centre point, but there are many variations.

Working with mandalas, whether you draw your own or colour in one that has already been created, can be a very relaxing and a surprisingly meditative exercise. You can find lots of free mandalas to download on the internet and colour, but also have a go at creating your own mandala for this month or for a particular goddess.

Pop on some quiet music, get your crayons out, release your inner child and allow yourself to be drawn into the mandala creation...you might be surprised what inspirations you find...

Once your mandala is finished, pop it on your altar.

Spirit Doll

Spirit dolls, poppets, goddess dolls...lots of different names from different cultures, but we thought it would be interesting to create a spirit doll, poppet or goddess representation for each month. Use whatever materials you have to hand or find easiest to work with – felt, cloth, string, Fimo, modelling clay...get creative.

Channel the energy of this month into your creation or add the characteristics and symbols of your chosen goddess.

If you make a doll from felt or material you can add herbs, spices and crystals to the inside too. If you work with clay or Fimo you can also incorporate herbs and crystals into the design.

The finished dolls will carry your very own magical energy with them together with the spirit of the month or the goddess you intended. Keep them on your altar.

Goddess Beauty

Lavender and Rosemary Shampoo

> 1 tablespoon dried lavender
> 1 tablespoon dried rosemary
> 30ml (1fl oz) liquid castile Soap
> 284ml (½ pint) hot water
> 1 teaspoon carrier oil such as sweet almond or olive oil (if hair is dry)

Add the herbs to a pan of boiling water. Take off heat and leave it to steep for about an hour.

Strain the water into a bottle. An old shampoo bottle is perfect.

Add the liquid castile soap and the carrier oil. Don't be alarmed if the colour of the water changes. Gently swirl around to mix.

To use, pour straight onto your hair and massage into your scalp. Rinse and dry your hair as normal.

Goddess Gift

The divine provides us with gifts...and we encourage you to step outside and see what the goddess, the divine, Mother Nature, has gifted you with.

It might be a feather, a pebble, a shell or maybe a leaf from a tree. Whatever you are gifted with you can add to your altar or maybe, if you are feeling artistic, you could create something with it.

A twig becomes a wand, a shell becomes a pendant, a feather becomes a smudge fan...think outside the box.

Medicine Bag

We have goddess medicine bags that we work with, just a square of material tied with a piece of thong, but inside we have representations of each goddess we have worked with. It helps us to keep a record of our journey, but also provides a focus for meditation and spiritual workings.

If you would like to create your own you can use a square of fabric. A bag made from felt or fabric works well too.

Each time you work with a different goddess ask them what symbol you should use to represent them in your medicine bag...you may be surprised.

By the end of this course you will have a wonderful collection of spiritual goddess items to keep in your own medicine bag.

Meditation Beads

Your mind can sometimes tend to wander when you are meditating, which leads to a loss of concentration. For practising meditation, meditation beads can act as a kind of 'anchor', or grounding point, enabling you to focus better. This can be extremely useful, especially if you are feeling tired when you meditate.

Conversely, if your mind is too active and over-energised, meditation beads will prevent you from becoming distracted or daydreaming. And, because the beads are moved in rhythm with your breathing, it helps you maintain your concentration.

At the end of this course you should have your own set of personal deities so you could create a string of meditation beads using one bead for each of your deities. It could be in the form of a necklace containing a bead for each of your twelve goddesses or you could make individual bracelets or pendants, one for each month.

The beads don't need to be used solely for meditation, you can use them throughout the day. When you awake, hold the beads and run them through your fingers and connect with their energy. This will set you up with positive intentions for the day.

Carry the beads with you in your pocket or bag, take them out during the day to remind you to stay grounded and focus on your tasks. Trust me, I need these all the time for focusing!

Hold the beads when you feel stressed or spacey to help bring you back centred and calm.

Finish your day the way you started by running the beads through your fingers and count your blessings. Release the negative points from your day and allow them to be replaced by the positive. Feel the good energy from the fabulous points of your day wash over you.

You also don't need to spend huge amounts of money. There are some beautiful meditation beads out there (often called prayer beads or malas), but you can make them yourself with whatever beads you have. There is no need to create a set of beads using expensive natural stones (although they are beautiful and full of natural energy). If all you have are wooden or plastic beads then use them, raid your children's play box even! The idea of the beads is to use them as a focus so even if you have a string of dried peas the intention is the same.

Feasting

We have included a recipe for each month – basically we don't need any excuse to include a cake recipe...but if you feel inclined to pop into the kitchen to bake we have given monthly suggestions on cakes to use in ritual to honour the goddess or just because they are yummy. If you love to cook you don't have to stop at cake, you could create a meal in honour of the goddess you are working with for the month (or just order a takeaway).

Lemon and Blueberry Cake

225g (8oz) butter, softened
225g (8oz) sugar
4 large eggs
225g (8oz) self raising flour
2 level teaspoons baking powder
Zest of two lemons
200g (7oz) lemon curd
350g (12oz) mascarpone
Punnet of blueberries

Preheat the oven to 180C/Gas 4. Lightly grease two 8inch sandwich tins and line the base with baking parchment.

Pop the butter, sugar, eggs, flour, lemon zest and baking powder into a bowl and beat for a couple of minutes until blended.

Divide the mixture between the prepared tins and level the surface. Bake for about 25 minutes until well risen and golden. Leave the cakes to cool for a couple of minutes in the tin before turning out onto a wire rack, then leave to cool completely.

Make the filling: whisk the lemon curd and mascarpone together until thick then chill until needed.

Lay one of the cakes on your serving plate and fill with half of the curd and mascarpone mix. You can pipe this or spread it with a knife, sprinkle with a handful of blueberries then put the other half of the cake on top. Spread or pipe the remaining mascarpone mix on top of the cake and decorate it with more blueberries.

October

My favourite time of the year and it isn't just because October includes Samhain...honest! I love the autumn, the crisp fresh air, the crunch of leaves under foot and the beautiful colours of the trees and fields. Oh and of course sitting indoors on a dark evening, curtains closed, sofa, blanket and a good book, having just scoffed a big bowl of casserole and dumplings...bliss.

To me this is a time to work on one's inner self, a time of hibernation. Take the time out to spend with *you*.

Meditate and work with your divination tools. Take a look at what worked for you over the past twelve months and what didn't, do a personal MoT check. Take a good look...what is in your reflection?

With the arrival of Samhain comes the thinning of the veil between the worlds, a time to remember those who have passed over and to raise a glass to our ancestors.

There is a theme of death at this time of the year.

The last harvest is taken in and the plants start to wither and die, but what they are actually doing is taking shelter to conserve and rebuild their energies to store them over the winter so that they are ready to be reborn in the spring.

Deities

In this part of the course we suggest nine goddesses that we associate with this month, have a read through the information and see if any of them resonate with you, it may be that one of them comes to you in the meditation, it might be that another deity altogether greets you...go with your intuition. We have also included a list of some deities that have celebrations or feast days within this month too.

Aida Wedo

A Caribbean goddess of rainbows, Aida Wedo appears as the rainbow python, a serpent whose scales are iridescent. Her snake body wraps around the earth and the seas, bringing protection and the linking of the power of heaven to the earth. She rules water, wind, fire, rainbows, fertility and serpents. Aida Wedo teaches her people about integrity, strength and integration of the mind, body and spirit. She is traditionally offered rice, eggs and milk. Her colour is white.

Aphrodite

Greek goddess of love and war, and goddess of sexual passion, love, pleasure and physical beauty. She rules marriages and the love that holds them together, but is also the goddess of illicit affairs. She teaches about dedication and self love, but she is also known to have a quick and occasionally unscrupulous response to any requests. Her symbols are the ocean, doves, apples, roses and mirrors.

Arnamentia

Arnamentia was a Celtic goddess of flowing water, spiritual healing and purification. She rules all bodies of water including springs and rivers. In times of need she offers renewal of the mind, body and soul.

Oba

Oba is a Yoruban goddess of rivers; she forms a triad with Oshun and Oya. Oba is the power of the flowing water representing the flow of time and life and the movement of energy. Call on Oba for protection, manifestation, movement, energy, restoration and flexibility. Turn to her for assistance when you need to 'go with the flow' or require inspiration.

Yemaya

An Orisha, an African goddess of water, Yemaya is honoured as the mother of the sea and the moon. She is the keeper of the female mysteries and a guardian of women. She aids in the conception of children and their births, protecting and blessing infants until they hit puberty. She is a healing goddess, showing compassion and kindness to those in need. Yemaya is the personification of rivers and bodies of water and is sometimes depicted as a mermaid.

Vivienne

A powerful sorceress and, to be honest, a bit power hungry, she used any means she could to get what she wanted. She is often associated with the Lady of the Lake in the Arthurian legends and said to have escorted Arthur to the Isle of Avalon at his death. She can work with you in sex or couples magic and also to warn about using manipulation...

Anuket

An Egyptian river and agriculture goddess associated with the river Nile. Her waters feed the fields, providing prosperity and abundance. She is also a patron of the poor and those in need.

Juturna

A Roman goddess of water, fire, fate, divination, protection and balance, she was often associated with wells and fountains. She can be called upon also to help put out emotional fires. Work with Juturna when using smoke divination.

Styx

A Greek goddess of the underworld and the river Styx, she is one of the Titan generation of Okeanides. She is associated with hatred. The river Styx flowed forth from the underworld with corrosive waters.

Feast/Celebration Days:

We have listed here the feast and celebration days for deities (we have included gods as well as goddesses) throughout October from various cultures and pantheons. These are taken from our own research...we apologise for any errors, but history is a fickle thing and calendars have changed over the years...

4th October

Ieiunium Cereris: 'Fast of Ceres'. This fast was held to honour the Roman goddess Ceres. It was originally held every five years, but was held every year by the time of the Empire.

5th October

Mania: These Roman festivals were held to placate the Manes. It was believed that on these days the Mundus, the passageway to the underworld, was open and the spirits of the dead were free to roam the earth.

7th October

Oschophoria: Dedicated to the Greek god Dionysus, this involved a procession led by two men dressed as women in commemoration of the two youths who Theseus disguised as maidens to protect the other maidens. They carry vine branches still bearing grapes and the procession starts at the temple of Dionysus and arrives at the shrine of Athena Skira to recall both Theseus' return and the death of Dionysus, by which he is reborn.

Pyanepsia: The rite involved hanging a mixture of pulses and a branch of olive or laurel on the gate of the temple of Apollo in Greece. The Athenian hero Theseus was said to have begun this ritual to thank Apollo and commemorate his victory over the Minotaur. Children carried a wand of laurel and went from house to house singing. Gifts were given to the children, which they exchange for the wands to bring the household good luck.

8th October

Festival of High Places: Chinese festival for good luck.

9th October

Amun: Ancient Egyptian festival for Amun, according to the festival list of Thutmose III at Elephantine.

11th-13th October

Thesmophoria: A three-day festival in various parts of Greece. Women participating in the autumn sowing festival had to fast and observe their chastity for several days. Married women would take supplies up to the top of the hill Thesmorphorion for two nights. They would build shelters made with plants. The second day they would fast. On the third day there would be a torch-lit procession to celebrate Demeter and her search for Persephone. A feast was then held and offerings to Demeter made in the hope of a good harvest.

11th October

Meditrinalia: This Roman agricultural festival was sacred to Meditrina and to Jupiter, and had something to do with the year's new wine.

13th October

Fontinalia: 'Feast of the Source'. During this Roman festival, garlands were thrown into springs and on top of wells to honour the god Fons.

13th October-11th November

Nine Emperor Gods: The first nine days of the 9th lunar month is the Nine Emperor Festival in China and the most visible signs of this festival are devotees dressed in white with a yellow cloth tied around their waist. The Nine Emperors are generally thought to be nine stars around the Big Dipper constellation and children of female deity Dou Mu. Seven of the stars are visible while two are invisible stars.

15th October
Ludi Capitolini: 'Capitoline Games'. The Ludi Capitolini were games held in honour of Jupiter Capitolini in Ancient Rome, and were only celebrated by his priests. They may have originally been held to honour Jupiter Feretrius.

15th October
Mars: Roman festival of Mars, god of war.

19th October
Armilustrium: This day marked the end of the Roman military campaign season. It was sacred to the god Mars.

22nd-23rd October
Oya festival: Celebrations of the Caribbean Orisha of the Wind, patron of the flooding of the Oya river and guardian of the gateway between life and death. It marks the onset of autumn and the dry season.

28th October
Baal: Ancient Phoenician festival of sun god Baal, god of nature and fertility.
Isis: Ceremonies for the Egyptian goddess Isis started.

29th October-2nd November
Winternights: The beginning of the winter season for the northern folk. Remembrance of the dead and one's ancestors was done during this feast. Winternights was a ceremony of wild abandon and it marked the end of the summer season of commerce and travel and the beginning of the winter season of hunting. Much divination was done during Winternights to

foretell the fates of those entering the coming year. It was said that if one sat on a barrow-mound (grave) all night long on Winternights, one would have full divinatory, shamanic (galdr and seith), and bardic (skaldr) powers...that is, if one retained one's sanity. Winternights marked the beginning of the Wild Hunt, which would continue until Walpurgisnacht. This festival corresponds roughly to the Celtic Samhain, and the modern American festival of Halloween, although the darker aspects of the festival are not as pronounced among the Norse people.

30th October

Anuqet: Local Elephantine festival of Anuqet according to the festival list of Thutmose III at Elephantine.

31st October

Samhain/All Hallows Eve: Samhain (pronounced SOW-in, SAH-vin, or SAM-hayne) means 'End of Summer', and is the third and final harvest festival in the old Irish year. The dark winter half of the year commences on this Sabbat. It is generally celebrated on 31st October, but some traditions prefer 1st November. It is one of the two 'spirit-nights' each year, the other being Beltane. It is a magical interval when the mundane laws of time and space are temporarily suspended, and the veil between the worlds is lifted. This was the time that the cattle and other livestock were slaughtered for eating in the ensuing winter months. Any crops still in the field on Samhain were considered taboo, and left as offerings to the nature spirits. Bonfires were built, (originally called bone-fires, for after feasting, the bones were thrown in the fire as offerings for healthy and plentiful livestock in the new year) and stones were marked with people's names. Then they were thrown into the fire, to be retrieved in the morning. The condition of the retrieved stone foretold that person's fortune in the coming year. Hearth fires were also lit from the village bonfire to ensure unity, and the ashes were spread over the harvested fields to protect and bless the land. To witches, Samhain is one of the four Greater Sabbats, or cross-quarter days. Because it is the most important holiday of the year, it is sometimes called 'The Great Sabbat'.

Not only is Samhain the end of autumn; it is also, more importantly, the end of the old year and the beginning of the new. It is Celtic New Year's Eve, when the new year begins with the onset of the dark phase of the year, just as the new day begins at sundown. The two themes, celebrating the dead and divining the future, are inexorably intertwined in Samhain.

Shigidi Festival: Veneration of the Orisha of Nightmares and the unknown dead of the African people. It involved a solemn parade by candlelight for unsettled spirits and ghosts.

Mahalya: Mahalaya is an auspicious occasion observed seven days before the Durga Puja, and heralds the advent of Durga, the goddess of supreme power. It is a kind of invocation or invitation to the mother goddess to descend on earth – 'Jago Tumi Jago'. This is done through the chanting of mantras and singing devotional songs.

Nava-ratri: 'Nava-ratri' literally means 'nine nights'. This Hindu festival is observed twice a year, once in the beginning of summer and again at the onset of winter. During Navaratri, Hindus invoke the energy aspect of god in the form of the universal mother, commonly referred to as 'Durga', which literally means the remover of miseries of life. She is also referred to as 'Devi' (goddess) or 'Shakti' (energy or power). It is this energy that helps the god proceed with the work of creation, preservation and destruction. In other words, you can say that god is motionless, absolutely changeless, and the Divine Mother, Durga, does everything. Truly speaking, worship of Shakti re-confirms the scientific theory that energy is imperishable. It cannot be created or destroyed. It is always there.

Lakshmi: On the full moon night following Dusshera or Durga Puja, Hindus worship Lakshmi ceremonially at home, pray for her blessings, and invite neighbours to attend the puja. It is believed that on this full moon night the goddess herself visits the homes and replenishes the inhabitants with wealth.

Karwa Chauth: 'Karwa Chauth' is a ritual of fasting observed by married Hindu women seeking the longevity, well-being and prosperity of their husbands. It is popular among married women in the northern and western parts of India, especially, Haryana, Punjab, Rajasthan, Uttar Pradesh and Gujarat. This festival comes nine days before Diwali on 'kartik ki chauth', i.e., on the fourth day of the new moon immediately after Dusshera, in the month of 'Karthik' (October-November). The term 'Chauth' means the 'fourth day' and 'Karwa' is an earthen pot with a spout – a symbol of peace and prosperity – that is necessary for the rituals. Hence the name 'Karwa Chauth'. Married women keep a strict fast and do not take even a drop of water. They get up early in the morning, perform their ablutions, and wear new and festive raiments. Shiva, Parvati and their son Kartikeya are worshipped on this day along with the ten karwas (earthen pots) filled with sweets. The karwas are given to daughters and sisters along with gifts.

Dhanteras: The Hindu festival of Dhanteras falls in the month of Kartik (October-November) on the thirteenth day of the dark fortnight. This auspicious day is celebrated two days before the festival of lights, Diwali. On Dhanteras, Lakshmi – the goddess of wealth – is worshiped to provide prosperity and well being. It is also the day for celebrating wealth, as the word 'Dhan' literally means wealth and 'Tera' comes from the date 13th. In the evening, the lamp is lit and Dhan-Lakshmi is welcomed into the house. Alpana or Rangoli designs are drawn on pathways including the goddess' footprints to mark the arrival of Lakshmi. Aartis, or devotional hymns, are sung eulogizing goddess Lakshmi and sweets and fruits are offered to her. Hindus also worship Lord Kuber as the treasurer of wealth and bestower of riches, along with goddess Lakshmi on Dhanteras. This custom of worshipping Lakshmi and Kuber together is in prospect of doubling the benefits of such prayers. People flock to the jewellers and buy gold or silver jewellery or utensils to venerate the occasion of Dhanteras. Many wear new clothes and wear jewellery as they light the first lamp of Diwali, while some engage in a game of gambling.

Deepawali or Diwali: Certainly the biggest and the brightest of all Hindu festivals. It is the festival of lights (deep = light and avali = a row i.e., a row of lights) that's marked by four days of celebration. Each of the four days in the festival of Diwali is separated by a different tradition, but what remains true and constant is the celebration of life, its enjoyment and goodness. Historically, the origin of Diwali can be traced back to ancient India, when it was probably an important harvest festival. However, there are various legends pointing to the origin of Diwali or 'Deepawali'. Some believe it to be the celebration of the marriage of Lakshmi with Lord Vishnu. In Bengal the festival is dedicated to the worship of Mother Kali, the dark goddess of strength. Lord Ganesha, the elephant-headed god, the symbol of auspiciousness and wisdom, is also worshipped in most Hindu homes on this day. In Jainism, Deepawali has an added significance to the great event of Lord Mahavira attaining the eternal bliss of nirvana. Diwali also commemorates the return of Lord Rama along with Sita and Lakshman from his fourteen-year-long exile and vanquishing the demon-king Ravana. In joyous celebration of the return of their king, the people of Ayodhya, the Capital of Rama, illuminated the kingdom with earthen diyas (oil lamps) and burst crackers. Each day of Diwali has its own tale, legend and myth to tell. The first day of the festival Naraka

Chaturdasi marks the vanquishing of the demon Naraka by Lord Krishna and his wife Satyabhama. Amavasya, the second day of Deepawali, marks the worship of Lakshmi, the goddess of wealth in her most benevolent mood, fulfilling the wishes of her devotees. Amavasya also tells the story of Lord Vishnu, who in his dwarf incarnation, vanquished the tyrant Bali, and banished him to hell. Bali was allowed to return to earth once a year, to light millions of lamps to dispel the darkness and ignorance, and spread the radiance of love and wisdom. It is on the third day of Deepawali — Kartika Shudda Padyami that Bali steps out of hell and rules the earth according to the boon given by Lord Vishnu. The fourth day is referred to as Yama Dvitiya (also called Bhai Dooj) and on this day sisters invite their brothers to their homes.

Apaturia: Apaturia was a Greek festival celebrated in Athens and nearly all other Ionian towns. Apaturia is unique among Greek festivals in being associated with a particular social group: the phratry, or brotherhood. The name probably means festival of 'common relationship'. The phratries celebrated Apaturia annually for three days in the month of Pyanopsion (October-November). The main function of the festival was to enrol new phratry members, who thereby acquired a title to citizenship. The first day of the festival, Dorpia (dinner), featured an evening meal. The central ritual of the second day, Anarrhysis (drawing back [of animals' necks]), was sacrifice to Zeus Phratrios and Athena Phratria.

Meditation

Take a deep breath in through your nose and a long sigh out through your mouth. Feel any tension in your body start to melt away as you become comfortable and relaxed. Take another breath in through your nose, the air going deep into your stomach, then slowly and gently release the breath out through your mouth.

Your everyday thoughts and worries fade away as you bring your attention solely to your breath as it moves gently in and slowly out. The world around you starts to dissipate and as it slips away you open your mind's eye to find yourself at the edge of a lake. It is early evening and the water looks so inviting, so you decide to take a dip. You remove your clothes and hang them on a nearby tree branch and step slowly into the lake. The water is a little cold, but it is welcoming to soothe your aching muscles.

You swim into the centre of the forest lake and dive down into the water. Once beneath the surface you open your eyes and are surprised that you can see everything in crystal-clear detail despite the fading light above. You see the roots of the water plants and swim through them freely.

Underneath the water the lake seems much bigger than it does from above. You are wondering about this when you notice what looks to be female figure swimming towards you. The top half of her body is definitely female, but her bottom half is made up of fins and scales. A mermaid!

She smiles at you and indicates for you to follow her. She swims deeper into the lake and you worry that you won't have enough breath. But you realise that under this water you don't need oxygen for some reason and so you follow deeper and deeper without fear.

You follow the mermaid along an underwater tunnel and out into a pool. You reach the surface, expecting to be gasping for air, but you are comfortable. You swim over to the edge of the pool and climb out and the mermaid follows you this time. As she climbs out you are amazed to witness her mermaid tail immediately transform into legs.

You are both standing in an underground cavern and you realise that you are in the presence of the Lady of the Lake and she has a special message for you.

She finishes her message and it is time for her to go, but she gives you a gift as a reminder of your swim through her lake together. She then bids you farewell before diving back into the pool. As you watch the ripples on the surface of the water you slowly start to become aware of your breath as it slowly moves in and out.

You gradually become aware of your surroundings again. Give your fingers and toes a wiggle.

Take your time and open your eyes when you are ready, make a drink, eat some chocolate (or other food if you cannot eat chocolate) to ground. Journal any messages the goddess gave you.

Energy/Spell Work

Communicating with ancestors and departed loved ones is easy at this time, for they journey through this world on their way to the Summerlands. It is a time to study the Dark Mysteries and honour the Dark Mother and the Dark Father, symbolised by the crone and her aged consort.

October is a good time to work magic for:

- Clearing
- Inner work
- Visualisation
- Banishing
- Psychic work
- Divination
- Planning new projects
- Manifestation
- Honouring your ancestors
- Balance
- Justice
- Removing blockages
- Ambition

Moon Lore

Our ancient ancestors tracked the passing of time by the phases of the moon. The full moon marking the start of the month, or moonth, and each lunation lasting approximately 29 days. Gradually each moon was given a name or a label, as we humans like to do. These names would be dictated by what was happening seasonally, like Seedfall Moon, or what activities were taking place – Harvest Moon or Hunter's Moon, for example. Unfortunately, there is no definitive list of names we can give, but throughout this course we will provide examples and more importantly we invite you to create your own list of names.

October's moon is often named Hunter's Moon as people would hunt and preserve as much meat and fruit during the shortening days as they could, to make sure they survived through winter. The Celts associate this moon with ivy, which teaches us strength and endurance. We look to the turning colours of the leaves as they fall from the trees given us the lessons of transformation, death and resurrection. In many ways October is the moon before the dark.

Names for the October Moon Include
Hunter's Moon, Blood Moon, Seed Fall Moon, Ivy Moon

In the Celtic Tree Calendar
Ivy Moon: 1st October-27th October; strength and endurance.
Reed Moon: 28th October-24th November; connection with the ancestors, looking within

During this month's full moon go outside if you can and soak up her energies, let her speak to you and see what names come to you.

Ritual
We believe that personal rituals should be...well personal! So we have given you an outline guide for your own ritual, but it is up to you to invoke the deity/deities of your choice, relevant to this month would be good because that's the idea of this course, but if someone else is shouting 'pick me, pick me' don't ignore them. Add in your own individual ideas and style and make the ritual your own.

- Cast the circle
- Call in the quarters
- Invoke deity
- Smudge
- Work some magic or divination or just sit quietly and meditate
- Feast...
- Thank and dismiss the quarters
- Thank and bid farewell to deity
- Close the circle
- And don't forget to ground!

Crystals

Crystals have often been associated with each month and/or the magical energy that the month brings. Try popping one in your pocket, on your altar or meditate with one this month. Again go with your intuition but here are some to get you started:

- Alexandrite
- Lilac kunzite
- Black obsidian
- Smoky quartz
- Jet
- Amber
- Citrine
- Topaz
- Garnet
- Pyrite
- Quartz
- Sandstone
- Gold
- Diamond
- Ruby
- Hematite

- Black, pink or green tourmaline
- Opal
- Lodestone

Our Favourite Gem for October – Smoky Quartz
Smoky quartz works to protect against negative energy, evil and bad luck of all kinds. It is also a good stone to work with to ease depression and to restore energy and positive thinking.

It helps to reduce anxiety and can aid with helping you to sleep and to keep away nightmares.

This stone offers total protection, whether you carry it on your person or place pieces of it around your home or in your car.

Focus on smoky quartz for astral travel, meditation and to channel earth energy.

Crystal Grid
You could use the energies of this month to make a crystal grid. Start with a crystal in the centre and add your intent, if it is for business success you could put a business card under the centre crystal then add crystals going around in a spiral or a mandala pattern fanning out from the centre. I like to add herbs and oracle or tarot cards to my crystal grids too. Once your intuition has told you what crystals to use and where to put them, visualise all the crystals, herbs and cards linking up with a 'web' of white light to bring your intent to reality.

Oil/Incense Blends
Create an essential oil or a loose incense blend to use when you are meditating or just to help you work with the energies of this month. Here are some herbs and scents for incense that we associated with this month, but go with your own ideas:

- Mugwort

- Catnip
- Mandrake
- Oak
- Sage
- Allspice
- Chrysanthemum
- Apple
- Pear
- Hazel
- Thistle
- Pomegranate
- Nuts
- Pumpkin
- Basil
- Camphor
- Clove
- Frankincense
- Yarrow
- Ylang ylang
- Heliotrope
- Mint
- Nutmeg
- Myrrh
- Copal
- Heather
- Ginger

Our Favourite Herb for October – Mugwort (Artemisia vulgaris)
Mugwort is a very ancient herb for healing, magic and divination and is known to be protective to women and travellers.

The Latin name Artemisia comes from Artemis, the Greek moon goddess and patron of women, so it is an excellent herb to use for feminine energy and issues.

A bundle of mugwort placed under your pillow will bring

about peaceful sleep and aid with lucid dreams and astral travel. Mugwort makes a good alternative to sage in smudge sticks for cleansing and clearing. Carry mugwort with you to provide psychic protection and use in workings to increase your psychic powers.

Mugwort does not seem to be particularly favoured by the fae so if you want to keep them out hang a bunch over your threshold.

A wash made with mugwort (dried mugwort steeped in boiling water) can be used to cleanse your crystals and tools or added to your floor wash. Drink mugwort tea to help with your divination skills (but do not drink this if you are pregnant).

Place mugwort in your shoes to gain strength and stamina.

Essential Oil/Incense Recipe – Dark Goddess Incense
Mix together:

- 2 parts copal
- 1 part bay
- 1 part clove
- 1 drop red wine

Altar
We would love for you to create an altar for the month. Go with your heart, but think about what this month means to you, what the weather is like, what the magical energy represents and if a goddess came to you then a representation of her would be good too.

Go mad with all the Halloween decorations along with symbols of the last harvest such as gourds and apples. Good colours to use are red, gold, orange and black.

Mandala
Mandala is a Sanskrit word meaning circle and is a spiritual and

ritual symbol that represents the universe. A mandala will often have a square with four gates containing a circle with a centre point, but there are many variations.

Working with mandalas, whether you draw your own or colour in one that has already been created, can be a very relaxing and a surprisingly meditative exercise. You can find lots of free mandalas to download on the internet and colour, but also have a go at creating your own mandala for this month or for a particular goddess.

Pop on some quiet music, get your crayons out, release your inner child and allow yourself to be drawn into the mandala creation…you might be surprised what inspirations you find…

Once your mandala is finished, pop it on your altar.

Spirit Doll

Spirit dolls, poppets, goddess dolls…lots of different names from different cultures, but we thought it would be interesting to create a spirit doll, poppet or goddess representation for each month. Use whatever materials you have to hand or find easiest to work with – felt, cloth, string, Fimo, modelling clay…get creative.

Channel the energy of this month into your creation or add the characteristics and symbols of your chosen goddess.

If you make a doll from felt or material you can add herbs, spices and crystals to the inside too. If you work with clay or Fimo you can also incorporate herbs and crystals into the design.

The finished dolls will carry your very own magical energy with them together with the spirit of the month or the goddess you intended. Keep them on your altar.

Goddess Beauty

Green Tea and Pomegranate Toner

> 100ml (3½ fl oz) green tea
> 50ml (2fl oz) pomegranate juice
> 50ml (2 fl oz) spring water
> Bottle or mister bottle

Put a green tea bag in the hot water and allow it to steep. Meanwhile, pour pomegranate juice and spring water into the bottle and combine. Once green tea has cooled, remove the tea bag and also add it to the bottle. Apply it to your face with a cotton wool pad or ball. Or, if you are using a mister bottle, give your face a spritz (you might want to close your eyes first).

This keeps in refrigerator for up to two weeks.

Goddess Gift

The divine provides us with gifts…and we encourage you to step outside and see what the goddess, the divine, Mother Nature, has gifted you with.

It might be a feather, a pebble, a shell or maybe a leaf from a tree. Whatever you are gifted with you can add to your altar or maybe, if you are feeling artistic, you could create something with it.

A twig becomes a wand, a shell becomes a pendant, a feather becomes a smudge fan…think outside the box.

Medicine Bag

We have goddess medicine bags that we work with, just a square of material tied with a piece of thong, but inside we have representations of each goddess we have worked with. It helps us to keep a record of our journey, but also provides a focus for meditation and spiritual workings.

If you would like to create your own you can use a square of fabric. A bag made from felt or fabric works well too.

Each time you work with a different goddess ask them what symbol you should use to represent them in your medicine bag...you may be surprised.

By the end of this course you will have a wonderful collection of spiritual goddess items to keep in your own medicine bag.

Meditation Beads

Your mind can sometimes tend to wander when you are meditating, which leads to a loss of concentration. For practising meditation, meditation beads can act as a kind of 'anchor', or grounding point, enabling you to focus better. This can be extremely useful, especially if you are feeling tired when you meditate.

Conversely, if your mind is too active and over-energised, meditation beads will prevent you from becoming distracted or daydreaming. And, because the beads are moved in rhythm with your breathing, it helps you maintain your concentration.

At the end of this course you should have your own set of personal deities so you could create a string of meditation beads using one bead for each of your deities. It could be in the form of a necklace containing a bead for each of your twelve goddesses or you could make individual bracelets or pendants, one for each month.

The beads don't need to be used solely for meditation, you can use them throughout the day. When you awake, hold the beads and run them through your fingers and connect with their energy. This will set you up with positive intentions for the day.

Carry the beads with you in your pocket or bag, take them out during the day to remind you to stay grounded and focus on your tasks. Trust me, I need these all the time for focusing!

Hold the beads when you feel stressed or spacey to help bring you back centred and calm.

Finish your day the way you started by running the beads through your fingers and count your blessings. Release the negative points from your day and allow them to be replaced by the positive. Feel the good energy from the fabulous points of your day wash over you.

You also don't need to spend huge amounts of money. There are some beautiful meditation beads out there (often called prayer beads or malas), but you can make them yourself with whatever beads you have. There is no need to create a set of beads using expensive natural stones (although they are beautiful and full of natural energy). If all you have are wooden or plastic beads then use them, raid your children's play box even! The idea of the beads is to use them as a focus so even if you have a string of dried peas the intention is the same.

Feasting

We have included a recipe for each month – basically we don't need any excuse to include a cake recipe...but if you feel inclined to pop into the kitchen to bake we have given monthly suggestions on cakes to use in ritual to honour the goddess or just because they are yummy. If you love to cook you don't have to stop at cake, you could create a meal in honour of the goddess you are working with for the month (or just order a takeaway).

Parsnip and Maple Syrup Cake

We are all familiar with the carrot cake, which was followed by the courgette cake and even the beetroot cake, but I had not tried parsnip cake...until recently...and I have to say it was incredibly moist, squishy and yummy.

175g (6oz) butter
250g (9oz) Demerara sugar
100ml (3½fl oz) maple syrup
3 large eggs

250g (9oz) self-raising flour
2 tsp baking powder
2 tsp mixed spice
250g (9oz) parsnips, peeled and grated
1 medium eating apple, peeled, cored and grated

Heat the oven to 180C/160C fan/gas 4. Grease 2 x 20cm sandwich tins and line the bases with baking parchment.

Melt the butter, sugar and maple syrup in a pan over gentle heat, and then cool slightly.

Whisk the eggs into this mixture, and then stir in the flour, baking powder and mixed spice, followed by the grated parsnip and apple.

Divide between the tins, then bake for 25-30 minutes until the tops spring back when pressed lightly.

Cool the cakes slightly in the tins before turning out onto wire racks to cool completely.

I filled the cake with caramel spread, but you could use butter cream or a cream cheese filling. I just topped it with an icing sugar and water mix then crumbled over some fudge.

November

Now we are the end of autumn and heading into winter. The last of the autumn leaves are falling from the trees and the smell of bonfires fills the evening air.

The evenings are dark as are the mornings, time to start the process of withdrawing and entering inwards. I think it is a bit of a dreary month for most.

November is a time for remembering, reaffirming relationships and giving thanks. This is the month of Guy Fawkes Night, when beautiful fireworks fill the skies. We gather round bonfires and eat jacket potatoes filled with cheesy beans.

There is also Remembrance Day, when we pay homage to those who fought in wars for us. Thanksgiving Day is celebrated in America and although we don't celebrate it in the UK, this marks the lead-up to and preparation for Yule and Christmas. I don't need an excuse to make a pumpkin pie either...

Deities
In this part of the course we suggest nine goddesses that we associate with this month. Have a read through the information and see if any of them resonate with you. It may be that one of them comes to you in the meditation, it might be that another deity altogether greets you...go with your intuition. We have also included a list of some deities that have celebrations or feast days within this month too.

Baba Yaga
Baba Yaga is a Russian hag goddess. She is the ancient witch who lives deep within the forests and is both feared and revered. She commands the spirits of the dead and is the keeper of wisdom. Baba Yaga is the guide to the shadow side of the self, teaching lessons needed for growth and expansion. She controls time and

the elements and will answer any question for those brave enough to ask.

Hecate

Hekate or Hecate is a witch goddess of Greece. Hecate is the crone aspect of the triple goddess, forming the triad with Persephone and Demeter, although she also appears as having three faces herself. She has power over heaven, earth and the underworld, and is often referred to as the Queen of Ghosts or the Guardian of the Spirit World. She brings protection to the world of spirits and ghosts and stops them from causing any harm. She is most often associated with the crossroads as a place of dark magic, wisdom and spiritual connection. She is a powerful sorceress and seer. Hecate shows her followers the pathway of witchcraft and helps those that seek it to find their inner self.

Nephthys

Nephthys is the sister of Osiris and Isis and the wife of Set. She is a very ancient goddess, first found in Old Kingdom Egyptian writings. She is often depicted riding in the funeral boat accompanying the dead into the Blessed Land. She is not exactly the personification of death, but she is the closest thing to it in Egyptian belief. She is believed to be the mother of Anubis, and thus stands at the head of an entire family of funerary deities. She is also revered as the head of the household of the gods, and her protection is given to the head woman of any house. In fact, her name is given as a title to such women (literally translated it means 'head of the house'). She also stands at the head of the bed to comfort women in childbirth.

Kali Ma

In the Hindu pantheon, Kali is a ferocious form of the Divine Mother, who sent her Shakti, the Mother Gauri, to free the gods from the dominion of the demonic forces Shumbh and Nishumbh who had conquered the three worlds of earth, the astral plane and the celestial plane. Kali is the goddess of time and the transformation that is death. Lord Shiva and Mother Gauri in their destructive form are known as Mahakala and Mahakali or Kali. Kali is the kundalini energy that paralyses the attachments produced by the solar and lunar currents. This attachment causes fear of death. In the ignorant one, she creates fear, while for others Kali removes the ignorance that makes us fear death, the basic insecurity of the first chakra, a fear rooted in the brain.

Maman Brigitte

In Vodou, Maman Brigitte (Grann Brigitte, Manman, Manman Brigit, Manman Brijit) is a death loa, the wife of Baron Samedi. Maman Brigitte is one of the few loa who is white and is depicted as being fair-haired and green-eyed with light European skin. She drinks hot peppers and is symbolised by a black rooster. Like Baron and the Ghede, she uses obscenities. She protects gravestones in cemeteries if they are properly marked with a cross.

Ishtar

Often equated with Innana, Ishtar is a Babylonian goddess of love, war, sexual love and royalty. Her power is at its height during the full moon and she brings strong fertile energy to those that seek it. She also brings protection and vengeance to women who have been wronged together with a pretty volatile temper.

Lilith

Lilith is thought to be the original Queen of Heaven. She rules elemental air, wind and storms and seduces men into the temples for sexual rites. In some tales, Lilith was claimed to be the first wife of Adam and merged with tales of witches and demons to explain her dominant nature. She has long been considered one of the first witches. She was represented as being the terrifying power that the Sumerians called Lamasthu and the Greeks Lamia, and is known by many other names. It is possible that Lilith was a form of the Babylonian goddess Ninlil. Lilith was described as a night demon, with a beautiful face, luxuriant hair and great wings; however, instead of feet she had talons.

Persephone

Daughter of the Greek goddess Demeter, she is a goddess of spring, growth and happiness. She also rules over agriculture and the innocence of youth. Her dark aspect is that of Queen of the Underworld and in this guise she brings the wisdom of life and death, but also magic and divination.

Nicneven

A Scottish goddess of protection, ghosts, divination, peace and winter, she is the crone goddess of Samhain. She looks after the realms of magic and witchcraft. In Scottish tales she is also the Queen of the Faeries.

Feast/Celebration Days

We have listed here the feast and celebration days for deities (we have included gods as well as goddesses) throughout November from various cultures and pantheons. These are taken from our own research…we apologise for any errors, but history is a fickle thing and calendars have changed over the years…

1st November

Pomonia: This Roman festival was held to honour Pomona, goddess of orchards.
Hathor: Egyptian festival for Hathor, according to the great festival list in the temple for Ramesses III at Medinet Habu.
Isis: The autumn festival of Isis lasted from three to five days.

Tea: The Assembly of Tara, the religious centre of Ireland, was under the patronage of the goddess Tea and took place on 1st November. There is a tradition in early Irish legends of holding a sacred feast on the shores of Lates.

6th November
Birthday of Tiamat: Babylonian festival.

10th November
Goddess of Reason Festival: The goddess of reason's themes are logic, reasoning, learning and the conscious mind. Her symbols are a crown of oak leaves (representing the seat of the divine). While this lady had no other specific designation other than the goddess of reason, she dispenses the power of knowledge to those who seek her. The French honoured this goddess with celebrations at Notre Dame, the world's most acclaimed centre of scholarship. Traditionally, the women depicting her wore a blue robe and red cap, then were crowned in laurel at the end of a procession. During the French Revolution, on 10th November 1793, a goddess of reason, most likely representing Sophia (wisdom), was proclaimed by the French Convention at the suggestion of Chaumette. As personification for the goddess, Sophie Momoro, wife of the printer Antoine-François Momoro, was chosen. The goddess was celebrated in Notre Dame de Paris. She was put on the high altar in the cathedral.

4th-17th November
Ludi Plebeii: 'Plebeian Games'. This set of Roman games was established in 220 BCE to honour Jupiter. They were opened with a procession of Rome's magistrates and priests that wound from the Capitoline through the Forum along the via sacra to the Circus Maximus. The first week of the games was set aside for plays and other types of theatre. The last three days were reserved for athletic events, and events in the Circus Maximus.

13th November
Festival of Jupiter: Roman festival.

18th November
Osiris: Start of the Khoiak ceremonies in honour of Egyptian god Osiris.

25th November
St Catherine: St Catherine of Sinai is celebrated on this day, a Christian version of Nemesis, goddess of the Wheel of Fate.

29th November
Saturnia: This festival honoured the sons of Saturn: Jupiter, Neptune, and Pluto.

Makahiki: The Makahiki festival punctuated the yearly farming cycle in ancient Hawaii. Celebrating harvest and Lono, the Hawaiian god associated with rain and fecundity, Makahiki marked a temporary halt to activities of war and occasioned lesser changes in many other daily routines. For religious reasons that coincided with seasonal weather, activities such as deep-sea fishing – associated with Ku, the god of war – were kapu, or prohibited, during Makahiki. Beginning in late October or early November when the Pleiades constellation was first observed rising above the horizon at sunset, the Makahiki period continued for four months, through the time of rough seas, high winds, storms and heavy rains. Makahiki was a time to gather and pay tithes to chiefs who redistributed the gifts of the land, a time to cease farming labours and a time to feast and enjoy competitive games. Hawaiians gave ritualised thanks for the abundance of the earth and called upon the gods to provide rain and prosperity in the future.

Skanda Sashti: Skanda Sashti is observed on the sixth day of the bright fortnight of the Tamil month of Aippasi (October-November). This day is dedicated to the second son of Lord Shiva – Lord Subramanya, also known as Kartikeya, Kumaresa, Guha, Murugan, Shanmukha and Velayudhan, who on this day, is believed to have annihilated the mythical demon Taraka. Celebrated in all Shaivite and Subramanya temples in South India, Skanda Sashti commemorates the destruction of evil by the Supreme Being. On this day, elaborate festivals are held with grandeur in South India. In many places the festival commences six days before the Sashti day and concludes on the day of the Sashti. During these days, devotees recite inspiring hymns, read stories of Subramanya, and enact the exploits of the lord on stage. Thousands of people gather for feasts, and massive amounts of camphor are burnt.

Bhai Dooj: After the high voltage celebrations of Diwali, the festival of lights and fire-crackers, sisters all over India get ready for 'Bhai Dooj' – when sisters celebrate their love by putting an auspicious tilak or a vermilion mark on the forehead of their brothers and perform an aarti of him by showing him the light of the holy flame as a mark of love and protection from evil forces. Sisters are lavished with gifts, goodies and blessings from their brothers. Bhai Dooj comes every year on the fifth and last day of Diwali, which falls on a new moon night. The name 'Dooj' means the second day after the new moon, the day of the festival, and 'Bhai' means brother. Bhai Dooj is also called 'Yama Dwiteeya' as it's believed that on this day, Yamaraj, the Lord of Death and the custodian of Hell, visits his sister Yami, who puts the auspicious mark on his forehead and prays for his well being. So it's held that anyone who receives a tilak from his sister on this day would never be hurled into hell.

According to one legend, on this day, Lord Krishna, after slaying the Narakasura demon, goes to his sister Subhadra who welcomes him with the holy lamp, flowers and sweets, and puts the holy protective spot on her brother's forehead.

Chhath Puja: Chhath Puja, also called Dala Puja, is a Hindu festival popular in the Northern and Eastern Indian states of Bihar and Jharkhand and even Nepal. The word 'Chhath' has its origin in 'sixth' as it is celebrated on the 6th day or 'Shasthi' of the lunar fortnight of Kartik (October-November) in the Hindu calendar – six days after Diwali, the festival of lights. Chhath is mainly characterised by riverside rituals in which the sun god or Surya is worshipped, giving it the name of 'Suryasasthi'. It underpins the belief that the sun god fulfils every wish of those living on earth, and so it's our duty to thank the sun with a special prayer for making our planet go round and bestowing living beings with the gift of life. The ghats or riverbanks throng with devotees as they come to complete their ritual worship or 'arghya' of the sun – both at dawn and dusk. The morning 'arghya' is a prayer for a good harvest, peace and prosperity in the new year and the evening 'arghya' is an expression of thanks to the benevolence of the sun god for all that he has bestowed during the year gone by.

The Cailleach: The three months of winter from Samhain to Brigantia were under the power and government of the Cailleach.

Meditation
Take a deep breath in through your nose and a long sigh out through your mouth. Feel any tension in your body start to melt away as you become comfortable and relaxed. Take another breath in through your nose, the air going deep into your stomach, then slowly and gently release the breath out through your mouth.

Your everyday thoughts and worries fade away as you bring your attention solely to your breath as it moves gently in and slowly out. The world around you starts to dissipate and as it slips away you open your mind's eye to find yourself at the edge of a lake. It is early evening and the water looks so inviting, so you decide to take a dip. You remove your clothes and hang them on a nearby tree branch and step slowly into the lake. The water is a little cold, but it is welcoming to soothe your aching muscles. You swim into the centre of the forest lake and dive down into the water. Once beneath the surface you open your eyes and are surprised that you can see everything in crystal clear detail despite the fading light above. You see the roots of the water plants and swim through them freely.

Underneath the water the lake seems much bigger than it does from above. Not seeming to need oxygen you swim through an underwater tunnel and out into a pool. You swim over to the edge of the pool and climb out.

You are standing in an underground cavern, alone and naked. You hear the gentle drip, drip, drip of water from the ceiling and splashing into the pool and the floor you are standing upon. Wondering where your journey will lead next you catch sight of a faint glow of orange at the far end of the cavern. It looks like a fire and so you make your way towards it.

As you draw nearer you see it is a small cooking fire. An old lady is cooking a meal in a cauldron over the flames. She is wearing a cloak with the hood pulled up so you cannot see her face. You are a bit wary to approach her, but you are also anxious to find a way out of the cavern and to your clothes.

As you approach the lady she draws the hood back from her cloak to reveal a very ancient, but wise face underneath. She smiles at you and says, 'All people return to me and from me they are reborn.'

This is the crone, goddess of life, death and rebirth. She shares a message that is just meant for you and gives you a gift.

You thank her and ask if she knows the way out. 'The only way is through my cauldron of rebirth,' she says. 'You must drink from it to be reborn.'

She hands you a cup and tells you to help yourself from the cauldron. You pull the ladle out of the cauldron and pour the liquid into your cup. You take a sip and the liquid is bitter but the crone urges you to drink more. And so you drink deep and the world around becomes dark. You become aware of your breath as it slowly moves in and out.

You slowly become aware of your surroundings again and give your fingers and toes a wiggle.

Take your time to open your eyes. When you are ready, make a drink, eat some chocolate (or other food if you cannot eat chocolate) to ground. Journal any messages the goddess gave you.

Energy/Spell Work

As the dark nights draw in November is a good time to work magic for:

- Clearing
- Freedom
- Release
- Relief
- Protection
- Inner work
- Visualisation
- Banishing
- Psychic work
- Divination
- Planning new projects
- Manifestation
- Honouring your ancestors
- Balance
- Justice
- Removing blockages
- Ambition

Moon Lore

Our ancient ancestors tracked the passing of time by the phases of the moon. The full moon marking the start of the month, or moonth, and each lunation lasting approximately 29 days.

Gradually each moon was given a name or a label, as we humans like to do. These names would be dictated by what was happening weather wise, like Snow Moon, Ice Moon or what activities were taking place – Harvest Moon or Hunting Moon, for example. Unfortunately, there is no definitive list of names we can give, but throughout this course we will provide examples and more importantly we invite you to create your own list of names.

November's moon brings us deeper into the colder months and at the edge of winter. It may bring snow and certainly will bring the first frosts. Outward growth has slowed and it is time to turn inward, to prepare for a slower time of inward growth and exploration.

Names for the November's Moon Include
Frosty Moon, Dark Moon, Tree Moon, Snow Moon, Mourning Moon

In the Celtic Tree Calendar
Reed Moon: 28th October-24th November; connection with the ancestors, looking within
Elder Moon: 25th November-23rd December; endings and beginnings.

During this month's full moon go outside if you can and soak up her energies, let her speak to you and see what names come to you.

Ritual
We believe that personal rituals should be...well personal! So we have given you an outline guide for your own ritual, but it is up to you to invoke the deity/deities of your choice, relevant to this month would be good because that's the idea of this course, but if someone else is shouting 'pick me, pick me' don't ignore them.

Add in your own individual ideas and style and make the ritual your own.

- Cast the circle
- Call in the quarters
- Invoke deity
- Smudge
- Work some magic or divination or just sit quietly and meditate
- Feast...
- Thank and dismiss the quarters
- Thank and bid farewell to deity
- Close the circle
- And don't forget to ground!

Crystals

Crystals have often been associated with each month and/or the magical energy that the month brings. Try popping one in your pocket, on your altar or meditate with one this month. Again go with your intuition but here are some to get you started:

- Black obsidian
- Brown zircon
- Silver sheen obsidian
- Smoky quartz
- Jet
- Amber
- Citrine
- Topaz
- Garnet
- Pyrite
- Quartz
- Sandstone
- Gold

- Diamond
- Ruby
- Hematite
- Black, pink or green tourmaline
- Opal
- Lodestone

Our Favourite Gem for November – Hematite
Polished hematite can be used as a magic mirror for divination purposes or to reflect back negative energy. This is an incredibly powerful stone to use for self healing and can draw out pain and illness. It can also bring about balance and calm.

The stone is helpful to use in disputes or arguments and to sort out any legal issues. It can also help dispel fear.

Use it for astral travel, but also to bring in psychic self defence, protection and grounding.

Crystal Grid
You could use the energies of this month to make a crystal grid. Start with a crystal in the centre and add your intent, if it is for business success you could put a business card under the centre crystal then add crystals going around in a spiral or a mandala pattern fanning out from the centre. I like to add herbs and oracle or tarot cards to my crystal grids too. Once your intuition has told you what crystals to use and where to put them, visualise all the crystals, herbs and cards linking up with a 'web' of white light to bring your intent to reality.

Oil/Incense Blends
Create an essential oil or a loose incense blend to use when you are meditating or just to help you work with the energies of this month. Here are some herbs and scents for incense that we associated with this month, but go with your own ideas:

- Mugwort

- Catnip
- Mandrake
- Oak
- Sage
- Allspice
- Chrysanthemum
- Apple
- Pear
- Hazel
- Thistle
- Pomegranate
- Nuts
- Pumpkin
- Basil
- Camphor
- Clove
- Frankincense
- Yarrow
- Ylang ylang
- Heliotrope
- Mint
- Nutmeg
- Myrrh
- Copal
- Heather
- Cumin
- Vanilla

Our favourite herb for November – Mint (Mentha spp, Mentha aquatic, Mentha piperita)
I have mint in my garden, but keep it restricted in a pot otherwise it would take over the world; you have been warned.

Use peppermint oil on your forehead and the corners of your books (yeah I know, I can't bring myself to put it on my books either) to aid concentration.

Drinking mint tea can help with keeping communications sweet. The scent is uplifting and positive and can also be used in travel spells. Mint can be cooling so I think it works well in spell work to 'cool down' a situation.

Add a few sprigs of fresh mint to a glass of water to cleanse and purify your body from the inside out. Add mint to your floor wash to clear and cleanse the home. Place peppermint leaves under your pillow for a calm and restful sleep. Keep a mint leaf in your purse or wallet to ensure money keeps coming in.

Peppermint has lots of cooling and calming medicinal properties so use it in healing spells too. Sprinkle mint around your property to provide protection from negative energy.

Essential Oil/Incense Recipe – Lift the Veil Incense
Mix together:

> 2 parts mugwort
> 1 part bay
> 1 part star anise

Use this in a well ventilated room.

Altar
We would love for you to create an altar for the month. Go with your heart, but think about what this month means to you, what the weather is like, what the magical energy represents and if a goddess came to you then a representation of her would be good too.

Your altar could perhaps start to represent the darker half of the year, but also continue with a hint of autumn left over...

Mandala

Mandala is a Sanskrit word meaning circle and is a spiritual and ritual symbol that represents the universe. A mandala will often have a square with four gates containing a circle with a centre point, but there are many variations.

Working with mandalas, whether you draw your own or colour in one that has already been created, can be a very relaxing and a surprisingly meditative exercise. You can find lots of free mandalas to download on the internet and colour, but also have a go at creating your own mandala for this month or for a particular goddess.

Pop on some quiet music, get your crayons out, release your inner child and allow yourself to be drawn into the mandala creation...you might be surprised what inspirations you find...

Once your mandala is finished, pop it on your altar.

Spirit Doll

Spirit dolls, poppets, goddess dolls...lots of different names from different cultures, but we thought it would be interesting to create a spirit doll, poppet or goddess representation for each month. Use whatever materials you have to hand or find easiest to work with – felt, cloth, string, Fimo, modelling clay...get creative.

Channel the energy of this month into your creation or add the characteristics and symbols of your chosen goddess.

If you make a doll from felt or material you can add herbs, spices and crystals to the inside too. If you work with clay or Fimo you can also incorporate herbs and crystals into the design.

The finished dolls will carry your very own magical energy with them together with the spirit of the month or the goddess you intended. Keep them on your altar.

Goddess Beauty

Peppermint Lip Balm

8 drops peppermint oil
2 tablespoons carrier oil (sweet almond is great)
1 tablespoon beeswax pellets
Glass dropper
Glass jar
Container (small pot, jar or tin)
Lipstick shavings (optional if you want a hint of colour)

Put the carrier oil and beeswax in the glass jar and put the lid on. Then place the jar in a pan of water and gently heat until the wax has melted and mixed nicely with the oil.

Carefully remove the jar from the pan of water and add 8 drops of peppermint oil. If you are using lipstick shavings to add a hint of colour then add those too.

Give the mixture a stir and immediately pour into your container and then leave to set for around 2 hours.

Goddess Gift

The divine provides us with gifts...and we encourage you to step outside and see what the goddess, the divine, Mother Nature, has gifted you with.

It might be a feather, a pebble, a shell or maybe a leaf from a tree. Whatever you are gifted with you can add to your altar or maybe, if you are feeling artistic, you could create something with it.

A twig becomes a wand, a shell becomes a pendant, a feather becomes a smudge fan...think outside the box.

Medicine Bag

We have goddess medicine bags that we work with, just a square of material tied with a piece of thong, but inside we have representations of each goddess we have worked with. It helps us to keep a record of our journey, but also provides a focus for meditation and spiritual workings.

If you would like to create your own you can use a square of fabric. A bag made from felt or fabric works well too.

Each time you work with a different goddess ask them what symbol you should use to represent them in your medicine bag...you may be surprised.

By the end of this course you will have a wonderful collection of spiritual goddess items to keep in your own medicine bag.

Meditation Beads

Your mind can sometimes tend to wander when you are meditating, which leads to a loss of concentration. For practising meditation, meditation beads can act as a kind of 'anchor', or grounding point, enabling you to focus better. This can be extremely useful, especially if you are feeling tired when you meditate.

Conversely, if your mind is too active and over-energised, meditation beads will prevent you from becoming distracted or daydreaming. And, because the beads are moved in rhythm with your breathing, it helps you maintain your concentration.

At the end of this course you should have your own set of personal deities so you could create a string of meditation beads using one bead for each of your deities. It could be in the form of a necklace containing a bead for each of your twelve goddesses or you could make individual bracelets or pendants, one for each month.

The beads don't need to be used solely for meditation, you can use them throughout the day. When you awake, hold the beads and run them through your fingers and connect with their energy. This will set you up with positive intentions for the day.

Carry the beads with you in your pocket or bag, take them out during the day to remind you to stay grounded and focus on your tasks. Trust me, I need these all the time for focusing!

Hold the beads when you feel stressed or spacey to help bring you back centred and calm.

Finish your day the way you started by running the beads through your fingers and count your blessings. Release the negative points from your day and allow them to be replaced by the positive. Feel the good energy from the fabulous points of your day wash over you.

You also don't need to spend huge amounts of money. There are some beautiful meditation beads out there (often called prayer beads or malas), but you can make them yourself with whatever beads you have. There is no need to create a set of beads using expensive natural stones (although they are beautiful and full of natural energy). If all you have are wooden or plastic beads then use them, raid your children's play box even! The idea of the beads is to use them as a focus so even if you have a string of dried peas the intention is the same.

Feasting

We have included a recipe for each month – basically we don't need any excuse to include a cake recipe…but if you feel inclined to pop into the kitchen to bake we have given monthly suggestions on cakes to use in ritual to honour the goddess or just because they are yummy. If you love to cook you don't have to stop at cake, you could create a meal in honour of the goddess you are working with for the month (or just order a takeaway).

Malteser Cake

  150g (5oz) butter, softened
  250g (9oz) sugar
  150g (5oz) self raising flour
  125g (4½oz) sour cream

4 medium eggs
50g (1½oz) cocoa powder
1 teaspoon baking powder
Pinch salt
½ teaspoon vanilla extract
100g (3½oz) dark chocolate
550g (19oz) icing sugar
250g (9oz) butter, softened
1 tablespoons milk
500g (17½oz) Maltesers (chocolate coated malted balls)

Preheat the oven to 180C/350F/Gas 4. Grease two 8 inch sandwich tins and line the bases with baking parchment.

Put the butter, sugar, flour, sour cream, eggs, cocoa powder, baking powder, vanilla extract and salt into a bowl then mix until smooth.

Divide evenly between the two tins and level the tops. Bake in the centre of the oven for 25-30 minutes.

Remove from the oven and leave to cool in the tins for a few minutes before turning out onto a wire rack to cool completely.

To make the butter cream, break the chocolate into pieces and microwave carefully (30 second blasts at a time) or in a bowl over a pan of simmering water until melted.

Sift the icing sugar into a bowl, add the butter and milk and beat until it is really light and fluffy. Then pour in the melted chocolate, stirring continuously.

Pop one of the cakes onto a serving plate then spread over a third of the butter cream. Sit the other sponge on top and spread the remaining butter cream all over the tops and sides of the complete cake. It doesn't need to be perfect as you are going to cover it with chocolate sweets.

Next you stick the Maltesers all over the cake...this is seriously boring but worth the effort! If you don't like Maltesers you could use chocolate buttons.

December

Chestnuts roasting on an open fire, Jack Frost nipping at your nose...oh I *love* this time of the year and I revert to being a complete child...

It is an absolute excuse for me to go into total cheesy festive decorating mode and of course baking lots of goodies, writing cards and wrapping presents... I really should have been Mrs Claus or should that be the Holly Queen?

So much of December and the winter solstice has been taken over with commercialism, sometimes it is hard to escape from it, but I like to focus on the theme of Yule as being a chance to reconnect with friends and spend time with family.

No matter where you live, whether it is in the middle of a snow-covered field surrounded by beautiful bare trees or whether you live in the middle of a city with the odd tree on the side of the road, you can still feel the magic in the air. The crisp cold mornings, the crunch of frost under foot and that silent feel that surrounds us, the earth is hibernating, waiting patiently to spring forth once again.

At the point of winter solstice the darkness reaches its height and as the wheel turns the sun begins to return, the days very slowly becoming longer. Winter is a time to draw inwards and reflect, to look back at the months that have passed before and to plan for the coming year.

The Holly King battles once more leaving behind the waning part of the year and gives way to the Oak King to rule the waxing months, a reminder that we are in a cycle and that rebirth must be preceded by death.

Yule is a time to celebrate with your friends and family and a good excuse to stuff yourself with mince pies, puddings, mulled wine and dried fruits...and chocolate...and cake...

Deities

In this part of the course we suggest nine goddesses that we associate with this month, have a read through the information and see if any of them resonate with you, it may be that one of them comes to you in the meditation, it might be that another deity altogether greets you...go with your intuition. We have also included a list of some deities that have celebrations or feast days within this month too.

Hel

Hel – Norse deity – daughter of Loki, ruler of Under-Earth, the Realm of Hel, and queen of the dead (except for the heroes and valiant ones who have a place with Odin at Valhalla). Hel controls the souls of the wicked and those who die of sickness or old age in her underground kingdom of Helheim. She is the dark hag who walks the line between life and death, and thins the veil between the worlds. It is Hel who gifts Odin his twin ravens of prophecy and wisdom. She is the patron of Nordic shamans. Usually she is depicted as half alive and half dead.

Holda

Holda is a winter goddess of northern Europe and is also called Snow Queen and Mother Holle. She brings prosperity to the good, but punishes the lazy. Holda is also a goddess of nature who controls the snow and fog. Often seen as a beautiful woman dressed in red and white, she is said to ride on the winds at Yule to deliver fortune and good health to those who honour her.

Skadi

Skadi is a giantess goddess from the Norse pantheon. Her name equates to the Old Norse noun meaning 'harm' or the Gothic/Old English word meaning 'shadow'. She lives in the mountains where the snow never melts and is a skilled huntress using her bow and arrow. Skadi rules the winter and the darkness that comes with it. She bestows justice and vengeance as necessary on those who do no good and is also the incarnation of righteous anger.

Black Annis

A hag and crone figure, bringer of death. Stories of her come from the myths and legends of Britain. She clawed a home for herself from a cave using her long sharp fingernails. She controls the seasons and the weather.

Sedna

An Inuit goddess of the underworld, she rules the depths of the ocean and all the creatures within it. Her father sacrificed her to the sea and her body was transformed into seals, whales and walruses. She is mother of the hunt and a goddess of endurance with power of life and death.

Frigga

A Norse mother goddess, she is the guardian of marriage and the household. A protector of women and children, she also brings the skills of divination and prophecy.

Pinga

A goddess of protection in the Inuit culture, she is a guardian of souls as well as being the goddess of the hunt.

Chione

Greek goddess of snow. She is the daughter of Boreas, the North Wind, and Oreithyia. She has a very icy temper and has no problem showing it. She is incredibly beautiful, but boy does she know it and she has the full on vanity to go with it.

Venus of Willendorf

A curvaceous female ornament found in an Ice Age camp in

Willendorf made from limestone rock called Oolite, which is composed of skeletons of tiny sea creatures. The surface of the stone had also been painted with red ochre. She reminds us that our ancestors worshipped the goddess in many forms.

Feast/Celebration Days:
We have listed here the feast and celebration days for deities (we have included gods as well as goddesses) throughout December from various cultures and pantheons. These are taken from our own research...we apologise for any errors, but history is a fickle thing and calendars have changed over the years...

1st *December*
Festival of Nehebkau: The Beginning of Eternity festival in Ancient Egypt.

2nd *December*
Shiva: Hindu festival of Shiva

5th *December*
Faunalia: A rural Roman festival held in honour of Faunus that involved eating, drinking, dancing, and sacrifices.

8th *December*
Neith: Egyptian festival of the goddess Neith.

10th *December*
Lux Mundi: This Roman festival honoured Libertas as the bringer of light into the world.
Goddess of Liberty Festival: French festival.

11th *December*
Septimontia/Septimontium: This festival was held to honour the Seven Hills of Rome, either all of them together, or just the

earliest enclosed part (inside the Servian Wall, which enclosed parts of the Caelian, Esquiline, Palatine, and Velian hills). During the festival sacrifices were made somewhere on each hill.

15th December
Alcyone: Greek festival.

17th December
Obaluaiye festival: Celebrations of the Orisha of work [business] and of the winter solstice.

17th-24th December
Saturnalia: An ancient Roman festival to honour the deity Saturn. The celebrations began with a sacrifice at the temple of Saturn, followed by banquets, exchanging of gifts and general partying. Masters would serve their slaves at the table and much general merriment was had by all. It was a festival of light leading towards the winter solstice and the renewal of the coming year.

18th December
Eponalia: This festival honoured the Celtic goddess Epona, who became popular with Romans. The Romans would celebrate on this day by giving all the horses, donkeys and mules a day of rest.

21st December
Winter Solstice/Yule: Winter Solstice occurs on 21st or 22nd December in the northern hemisphere. It refers to the shortest day of the year, when the least amount of sunlight reaches the earth. The term 'solstice' derives from the Latin words sol (sun) and sistere (to stand), meaning that the sun has reached its northernmost ecliptic and appears to stand still. Throughout history, many cultures and religions have marked this day with

festivals and rituals.

This is in celebration of the fact they have survived halfway through the winter (this holiday is sometimes called 'midwinter celebrations'). This was especially significant in northern European countries, where it was not always certain that food storage would last through winter months. To many societies, the winter solstice also symbolised the earth's regeneration or rebirth. From this day forward, the days would continually grow longer as sunlight increased.

Divalia: The Divalia honoured the Roman goddess Angerona in rites so secret that even the statue of the goddess had to be gagged in order to keep the details secret.

29th December

Festival of Raising the Willow: Egyptian festival, according to the great festival list in the temple for Ramesses III at Medinet Habu

Birthday of Ra: Egyptian festival honouring the god.

Meditation

Take a deep breath in through your nose and a long sigh out through your mouth. Feel any tension in your body start to melt away as you become comfortable and relaxed. Take another breath in through your nose, the air going deep into your stomach, then slowly and gently release the breath out through your mouth.

Your everyday thoughts and worries fade away as you bring your attention solely to your breath and as it moves gently in and slowly out the world around you starts to dissipate and slips away.

You open your mind's eye to find yourself in a winter landscape in the dead of night. All around you is a blanket of white snow for as far as your eye can see. It glitters and gleams in the moonlight like a carpet of crystals as you look out across the landscape.

As you walk you hear the gentle crunch of your footsteps in the snow and you see your breath as it hits the cold air. But other than you there

are no other sounds, it is as if the land is sleeping.

Then you hear a sound in the distance. It sounds like bells jingling and you look around to see where it is coming from. You see a sleigh coming in your direction. It is being pulled by reindeer and on the sleigh stands a woman. As she draws level with you she brings the reindeer to a stop and indicates for you to step aboard the sleigh with her.

Once you are on board the sleigh, the reindeer take off again starting with a fast run and then leaping off into the air. You are flying high above the tundra and there is snow-covered landscape for as far as the eye can see.

The woman on the sleigh tells you she is the goddess of the tundra and your goddess for December. Then she shares a message that is just for you.

When she finishes her message the reindeer start to descend and alight back on the snow. You step from the sleigh and the goddess gives you a gift to remind you of your sleigh ride together. Then she is off again into the sky on the reindeer-pulled sleigh and you find yourself alone again on the tundra. You start to become aware of your breath as it slowly moves in and out.

You slowly become aware of your surroundings again and give your fingers and toes a wiggle.

Take your time and open your eyes. When you are ready, make a drink, eat some chocolate (or other food) to ground and journal any messages the goddess gave you.

Energy/Spell Work

Magical energies at this time of the year are good for:

- Honouring family and friends
- Peace
- Personal renewal
- Meditation
- Dream work

- Balance
- Knowledge
- Loyalty
- True feelings
- Truth
- Clarity
- Transition
- Planning
- Long term projects

Moon Lore

Our ancient ancestors tracked the passing of time by the phases of the moon. The full moon marking the start of the month, or moonth, and each lunation lasting approximately 29 days. Gradually each moon was given a name or a label, as we humans like to do. These names would be dictated by what was happening weather wise, like Snow Moon, Ice Moon or what activities were taking place – Harvest Moon or Hunting Moon, for example. Unfortunately, there is no definitive list of names we can give, but throughout this course we will provide examples and more importantly we invite you to create your own list of names.

December is a moon of endings and beginnings. It brings us to the close of the calendar year, but it also gives us Yule and the promise of rebirth and lengthening days to come. December's moon can be draining as we fight our instincts to withdraw and hibernate with the expectations to be social and festive. Try to balance both if you can!

Names for the December's Moon Include
Cold Moon, Long Nights Moon, Moon before Yule, Snow Moon

In the Celtic Tree Calendar
Elder Moon: 25th November-23rd December; endings and

beginnings

Birch Moon: 24th December-20th January; new beginnings, goal setting, creativity and fertility

During this month's full moon go outside if you can and soak up her energies, let her speak to you and see what names come to you.

Ritual

We believe that personal rituals should be...well personal! So we have given you an outline guide for your own ritual, but it is up to you to invoke the deity/deities of your choice, relevant to this month would be good because that's the idea of this course, but if someone else is shouting 'pick me, pick me' don't ignore them. Add in your own individual ideas and style and make the ritual your own.

- Cast the circle
- Call in the quarters
- Invoke deity
- Smudge
- Work some magic or divination or just sit quietly and meditate
- Feast...
- Thank and dismiss the quarters
- Thank and bid farewell to deity
- Close the circle
- And don't forget to ground!

Crystals

Crystals have often been associated with each month and/or the magical energy that the month brings. Try popping one in your pocket, on your altar or meditate with one this month. Again go with your intuition but here are some to get you started:

- Cat's eye
- Ruby
- Diamond
- Garnet
- Bloodstone
- Emerald
- Alexandrite
- Kunzite
- Citrine
- Green tourmaline
- Blue topaz
- Pearl
- Clear quartz
- Lapis lazuli
- Smoky quartz

Our Favourite Gem for December – Pearl
Pearl is a stone of harmony and balance and can help you synchronise with the cycles of the moon and the seasons and is especially useful for women to help with their menstrual and hormonal cycles.

Use pearl to increase your spiritual energies and connection, it also brings harmony and peace to any person or place.

Pearl is a particularly good stone to use in prosperity and money spell work and it can also be used to break the connection between yourself and a destructive relationship.

Crystal Grid
You could use the energies of this month to make a crystal grid. Start with a crystal in the centre and add your intent, if it is for business success you could put a business card under the centre crystal then add crystals going around in a spiral or a mandala pattern fanning out from the centre. I like to add herbs and oracle or tarot cards to my crystal grids too. Once your intuition has told

you what crystals to use and where to put them, visualise all the crystals, herbs and cards linking up with a 'web' of white light to bring your intent to reality.

Oil/Incense Blends

Create an essential oil or a loose incense blend to use when you are meditating or just to help you work with the energies of this month. Here are some herbs and scents for incense that we associated with this month, but go with your own ideas:

- Bayberry
- Nutmeg
- Saffron
- Evergreen
- Moss
- Oak
- Sage
- Bay
- Cedar
- Frankincense
- Ginger
- Holly
- Ivy
- Juniper
- Mistletoe
- Myrrh
- Pine
- Rosemary
- Chamomile
- Cinnamon
- Valerian
- Yarrow
- Star anise
- Carnation

- Rose geranium

Our Favourite Herb For December – Cinnamon (Cinnamomum zeylanicum, Cinnamomum verum)
Such a fabulous scent and flavour packing a powerful punch of energy, cinnamon is made from the dried bark of the branches of the tree.

Burn cinnamon as an incense to bring focus and concentration. This will also bring about a deeper spiritual connection and boost your psychic abilities.

Add cinnamon to sachets and pouches to bring about love and success. I often add a pinch of powdered cinnamon to any spell work that needs an extra boost of power. That cinnamon power punch also gives you the strength and courage to make necessary changes in your life.

Tie a bundle of cinnamon sticks with a black or red ribbon and hang it in your hallway to bring protection, love and success to your household.

Wear a dab or two of cinnamon oil when you go on a date for added ooh la la. (It might be an idea to dilute this with a carrier oil first if your skin is sensitive).

Essential Oil/Incense Recipe – Winter Celebration Incense
Mix together:

   3 parts frankincense
   2 parts pine needles
   1 part juniper berries
   1 part cinnamon bark

Altar
We would love for you to create an altar for the month. Go with your heart, but think about what this month means to you, what the weather is like, what the magical energy represents and if a

goddess came to you then a representation of her would be good too.

For decorating an altar at this time of year I like to use lots of candles in reds, gold and greens, evergreens, holly, mistletoe, poinsettia, Yule log, wreaths, bells and heap loads of baubles and fairy lights.

Mandala

Mandala is a Sanskrit word meaning circle and is a spiritual and ritual symbol that represents the universe. A mandala will often have a square with four gates containing a circle with a centre point, but there are many variations.

Working with mandalas, whether you draw your own or colour in one that has already been created, can be a very relaxing and a surprisingly meditative exercise. You can find lots of free mandalas to download on the internet and colour, but also have a go at creating your own mandala for this month or for a particular goddess.

Pop on some quiet music, get your crayons out, release your inner child and allow yourself to be drawn into the mandala creation…you might be surprised what inspirations you find…

Once your mandala is finished, pop it on your altar.

Spirit Doll

Spirit dolls, poppets, goddess dolls…lots of different names from different cultures, but we thought it would be interesting to create a spirit doll, poppet or goddess representation for each month. Use whatever materials you have to hand or find easiest to work with – felt, cloth, string, Fimo, modelling clay…get creative.

Channel the energy of this month into your creation or add the characteristics and symbols of your chosen goddess.

If you make a doll from felt or material you can add herbs, spices and crystals to the inside too. If you work with clay or

Fimo you can also incorporate herbs and crystals into the design.

The finished dolls will carry your very own magical energy with them together with the spirit of the month or the goddess you intended. Keep them on your altar.

Goddess Beauty

Coconut Oil Body Butter

200g (7oz) coconut oil
A few drops of your favourite essential oil

Put the coconut oil and essential oil a mixing bowl. Take an electric food mixer and whisk on high speed for five minutes, or until whipped onto a light airy consistency.

Spoon the mixture into a clean jar and store at room temperature.

Goddess Gift

The divine provides us with gifts...and we encourage you to step outside and see what the goddess, the divine, Mother Nature, has gifted you with.

It might be a feather, a pebble, a shell or maybe a leaf from a tree. Whatever you are gifted with you can add to your altar or maybe, if you are feeling artistic, you could create something with it.

A twig becomes a wand, a shell becomes a pendant, a feather becomes a smudge fan...think outside the box.

Medicine Bag

We have goddess medicine bags that we work with, just a square of material tied with a piece of thong, but inside we have representations of each goddess we have worked with. It helps us to keep a record of our journey, but also provides a focus for meditation and spiritual workings.

If you would like to create your own you can use a square of fabric. A bag made from felt or fabric works well too.

Each time you work with a different goddess ask them what symbol you should use to represent them in your medicine bag…you may be surprised.

By the end of this course you will have a wonderful collection of spiritual goddess items to keep in your own medicine bag.

Meditation Beads

Your mind can sometimes tend to wander when you are meditating, which leads to a loss of concentration. For practising meditation, meditation beads can act as a kind of 'anchor', or grounding point, enabling you to focus better. This can be extremely useful, especially if you are feeling tired when you meditate.

Conversely, if your mind is too active and over-energised, meditation beads will prevent you from becoming distracted or daydreaming. And, because the beads are moved in rhythm with your breathing, it helps you maintain your concentration.

At the end of this course you should have your own set of personal deities so you could create a string of meditation beads using one bead for each of your deities. It could be in the form of a necklace containing a bead for each of your twelve goddesses or you could make individual bracelets or pendants, one for each month.

The beads don't need to be used solely for meditation, you can use them throughout the day. When you awake, hold the beads and run them through your fingers and connect with their energy. This will set you up with positive intentions for the day.

Carry the beads with you in your pocket or bag, take them out during the day to remind you to stay grounded and focus on your tasks. Trust me, I need these all the time for focusing!

Hold the beads when you feel stressed or spacey to help bring you back centred and calm.

Finish your day the way you started by running the beads through your fingers and count your blessings. Release the negative points from your day and allow them to be replaced by the positive. Feel the good energy from the fabulous points of your day wash over you.

You also don't need to spend huge amounts of money. There are some beautiful meditation beads out there (often called prayer beads or malas), but you can make them yourself with whatever beads you have. There is no need to create a set of beads using expensive natural stones (although they are beautiful and full of natural energy). If all you have are wooden or plastic beads then use them, raid your children's play box even! The idea of the beads is to use them as a focus so even if you have a string of dried peas the intention is the same.

Feasting

We have included a recipe for each month – basically we don't need any excuse to include a cake recipe...but if you feel inclined to pop into the kitchen to bake we have given monthly suggestions on cakes to use in ritual to honour the goddess or just because they are yummy. If you love to cook you don't have to stop at cake, you could create a meal in honour of the goddess you are working with for the month (or just order a takeaway).

Mincemeat Frangipane Tarts

500g (17½oz) sweet short crust pastry
300-350g (10-12oz) mincemeat
250g (9oz) butter (softened)
250g (9oz) caster sugar
5 medium eggs (beaten)
125g (4½oz) self raising flour
125g (4½oz) ground almonds

1 teaspoon almond extract
Icing sugar for dusting

Preheat the oven to 180c/gas mark 4. Line a baking tray with greaseproof paper.

On a floured surface, roll out the pastry in a rectangle a little smaller than your baking tin. Then lift the pastry into the tin and push it to the edges and corners until it completely covers the base. Blind bake the pastry for 8-10 minutes until it is a lovely golden colour.

While the pastry is still warm spoon the mincemeat onto the pastry and spread thinly.

Beat together the butter and sugar until pale and creamy. Beat in the eggs a little at a time, adding a tbsp of flour to prevent splitting or curdling. Fold in the almonds, flour and almond extract. Spoon over the mincemeat and spread evenly.

Bake for 30-40 minutes until golden and firm. Leave to cool. Remove from the tray and peel away the greaseproof paper. Cut it into 32 squares then dust lightly with icing sugar.

The Goddess Within...

Once you have worked for a full year through this course you will hopefully have your very own personal pantheon of goddesses to work with but ultimately the real magic is *within you*.

Know that you have the power and support to create your own destiny, *you* are the goddess.

Deities
You have your own twelve personal goddesses to call upon whenever you need them and they will be there for you.

Feast/Celebration Days
Any day of the week, celebrate being *you*.

Sacred Space Meditation
Take several deep breaths in and out...

As your world around you dissipates you find yourself in a place that feels very comfortable to you, it might be a room in a house or perhaps a castle even, it may be a spot in nature; in the woods or on the beach, but you know that it is your own personal space.

Look around you, walk around and see what is in your space...

If you feel it needs something added, maybe some furniture, divination tools or decoration of some sort then know that you can add it just with a thought...

What is the temperature like? Is it warm enough or cool enough? You can make the perfect climate...it is your space.

What sounds can you hear? Is there music or the hum of nature?

Are there any animals in your sacred space?

Is it light or dark? Is it daytime or night time? You are in control...

This is your own personal sacred space that you can visit during meditation at any time; you can also make changes at any point, and the space can grow with you.

Use the space to connect with your inner thoughts and feelings. Use the space to seek answers to questions or issues that need clarity. Use the space to just be…

When you are ready slowly come back to this reality, wriggling your fingers and toes and gently open your eyes, but know that the space you have created will always be there when you need it.

Energy/Spell Work

Work magic for *you*:

- Self confidence
- Self worth
- Self acceptance
- Self expression
- Self healing
- Self esteem
- Self sufficiency
- Inner power
- Inner peace
- Balance
- Emotions

Moon Phase

Most witches will have heard of or experienced the rite called Drawing down the Moon (you can draw down the sun too). This ritual supposedly dates back to the Dianic witches of Thessaly from Ancient Greece.

It is a powerful ritual and can be a very strong experience that can shed light on every aspect of your life and inner being. It can also open up your psychic abilities. This is my interpretation of the Drawing down the Moon ritual, there are more structured and ceremonial versions that can be found on the internet if you prefer. It is the art of drawing upon the power of the moon to send you into a trance and to channel the power of the goddess. In some covens or traditions the High Priestess will say the Charge of the Goddess (attributed to Doreen Valiente, but there are other versions) to invoke her, while in some traditions the Charge of the Goddess is spoken after the invocation, being the words of the goddess herself.

This ritual really needs to be performed outside as you need to be able to see the moon, the full moon is preferable. Even if the sky is full of clouds, the power of the full moon will still be available to you.

Cast a circle and call the quarters as you would do for any ritual. Then slowly start breathing in the light of the moon, filling your entire body with its moonbeams; make sure you do a bit of grounding through your feet to stop yourself from floating away though!

The purpose is to go into trance to enable the goddess to channel through you. This can be done by invocations to her, but I find that starting to slowly spin myself around, swirling and twirling while trying to keep an eye on the moon works well. When you come to a stop, the moon seems to rush down towards you. As the power of the moon enters your body you may get images or hear messages. These may be for you, but if you are in a group the messages may be for other members of the ritual. Speak out loud everything you hear and see whether it is words, symbols or images.

When the messages have stopped you can kneel on the ground and have a scrying bowl filled with water in front of you. Make sure the moonlight shines directly onto the water; you may then also get more images in the surface of the water.

When you have finished and closed your ritual make sure to ground properly.

You may want to write down all the messages as soon as you finish as they do have a tendency to escape from your memory quite quickly!

Arc of the Goddess Ritual

This ritual has been written to bring together the energies of all twelve of the goddesses.
Items needed:

A mirror
A candle
Seasonal cake or biscuit and a drink

Optional items:

Incense
Music
Colouring pens and paper

Cast the circle deosil (clockwise) saying:

I cast this circle first for the maiden who has bright and vibrant light illuminates where my path begins.
Twice I cast for the mother who gently supports and protects us as I find my own way.
A third time I cast for the matriarch who teaches me to journey through unseen worlds.
The forth and last time for the crone who gives me wisdom and strength to persevere.
By the power of the goddess this circle is cast.
So mote it be!

Light the candle, calling upon the goddesses of the arc:

I call to the Goddess of Earth, Guardian of the Land
She who is cold and dark and resting
Bring with you the calm and stillness of the land
Hail and welcome!

I call to the Maiden, the Creatrix of all Life
She who stirs the magical energies beneath the earth
Give me inspiration to create new ideas
Hail and welcome!

I call to the Goddess of Spring, Mountain Spirit
She of the awakening land
Bring with you new energies that stir the earth
Hail and welcome!

I call to the Goddess of Air, Bringer of the Breeze
She who cleanses and purifies
Grant me strength to face the winds of change
Hail and welcome!

I call to the Mother, Healer and Restorer
She who nurtures the earth and all the resides there
Teach me the gift of unconditional love
Hail and welcome!

I call to the goddess of Summer, Lady of the Meadows
She who brings the warmth of the solstice sun
Bring with you vitality and happiness
Hail and welcome!

I call the goddess of Fire, Keeper of the Flame
She who creates blazing passion and energy
Share with me the spark of divine inspiration
Hail and welcome!

I call to the Matriarch, Keeper of Wisdom
She her lifts the veil to the Otherworld
Show me the mysteries that are kept hidden
Hail and welcome!

I call to the Goddess of Autumn, Guardian of the Forest
She who brings change and transformation
Teach me to go with the ebb and flow of the season
Hail and welcome!

I call to the goddess of Water, Ladies of the Lake
She who builds strength from emotion
Sooth me with your watery depths
Hail and welcome!

I call to the Crone, Lady of Death and Destruction
She who burns away that which no longer serves
Give me to the strength to walk through your flames
Hail and welcome!

I call the goddess of Winter, Lady of the Tundra
She who is the stillness of the land ready for slumber
Guide me on my inner journey
Hail and welcome!

Feel these goddess energies as they share your circle and your heart. Breathe in the energies. All goddesses are one goddess and she dwells in you. Take the mirror and look at your reflection, see all the faces of the goddess looking back at you. See the goddess within you and smile because you are beautiful.

You may feel inspired to create, draw, write or just sit for a while in silent meditation or perhaps listen to some relaxing music. This is your time...just for you...

When you have allowed yourself enough time, finish the ritual by eating some of the food and drink to prepare yourself to close your circle. Don't forget to save some for offerings to leave outside.

To release the arc, say:

Goddesses of the Arc I thank you for the lessons and gifts you have brought to my circle today.
Stay if you will but return to your realms if you must.
Hail and farewell!

Walk the circle widdershins (anti-clockwise). Say:

This circle is open but like the love of the goddess it remains forever in my heart. Blessed be!

Crystals

Meditate and carry crystals that are personal to you and provide the energies that you need. Again go with your intuition but here are some to get you started...

- Calcite
- Rose quartz
- Moss agate
- Chrysoberyl
- Citrine
- Hematite
- Fuchsite
- Iron pyrites
- Opal
- Rhodocrosite
- Sodalite
- Kunzite
- Blue lace agate
- Blue tourmaline
- Larimar
- Sunstone
- Amber
- Jade

Oil/Incense Blends

Create your own anointing oil or incense blend just for *you*. Here are some herbs and scents that are associated with courage, happiness, health, love, luck, strength and peace but go with your own ideas...

- Borage
- Sweetpea
- Tea
- Thyme
- Yarrow
- Catnip
- Hawthorn
- Lavender
- Marjoram
- Meadowsweet
- Caraway
- Coriander
- Galangal
- Geranium
- Nutmeg
- Oak
- Tansy
- Allspice
- Heather
- Orange
- Poppy
- Rose
- Star anise
- Strawberry
- Vervain
- Bay
- Carnation
- Mugwort

Essential Oil recipe
Create your own personal recipe that is unique to you...

Altar
We would love for you to create an altar for *you*. This one is all about you, put personal representations on it, photos of you that you love, pieces of jewellery and anything that makes you smile and feel happy.

Mandala
Mandala is a Sanskrit word meaning circle and is a spiritual and ritual symbol that represents the universe. A mandala will often have a square with four gates containing a circle with a centre point, but there are many variations.

Working with mandalas whether you draw your own or colour in one that has already been created can be a very relaxing and surprisingly meditative exercise.

Pick one of the mandalas that you can find free on the internet to download or preferably create one that is all about *you*, make it your own personal mandala.

Pop on some quiet music, get your crayons out, release your inner child and allow yourself to be drawn into the mandala creation...you might be surprised what inspirations you find...

Once your mandala is finished pop it on your altar.

Spirit Doll
Spirit dolls, poppets, goddess dolls...lots of different names from different cultures. Use whatever materials you have to hand or find easiest to work with – felt, cloth, string, Fimo, modelling clay...get creative...

This one is a representation of you. Don't get too hung up on likeness or vanity...just be guided by your intuition...

If you make a doll from felt or material you can add herbs, spices and crystals to the inside too. If you work with clay or Fimo, you can also incorporate herbs and crystals into the design.

Goddess Gift

The divine provides us with gifts...and we encourage you to step outside and see what the goddess, the divine; Mother Nature...has gifted you with.

It might be a feather, a pebble, a shell or maybe a leaf from a tree. Whatever you are gifted with you can add to your altar or maybe if you are feeling artistic you could create something with it.

A twig becomes a wand, a shell becomes a pendant a feather becomes a smudge fan...think outside the box...

Medicine Bag

We have goddess medicine bags that we work with, just a square of material tied with a piece of thong, but inside we have representations of each goddess we have worked with. It helps us to keep a record of our journey, but also provides a focus for meditation and spiritual workings.

If you would like to create your own you can use a square of fabric, or a bag made from felt or fabric works well too.

Pop something into your medicine bag that represents you.

Meditation Beads

Your mind can sometimes tend to wander when you are meditating which leads to a loss of concentration. For practising meditation, meditation beads can act as a kind of 'anchor' or grounding point enabling you to focus better. This can be extremely useful especially if you are feeling tired when you meditate.

Conversely, if your mind is too active and over-energised, meditation beads will prevent you from becoming distracted or daydreaming. And, because the beads are moved in rhythm with your breathing, it helps you maintain your concentration.

At the end of this course you should have your own set of personal deities so you could create a string of meditation beads using one bead for each of your deities, it could be in the form of a necklace containing a bead for each of your twelve goddesses or you could make individual bracelets or pendants, one for each month. This one however is for *you*...create something in the colours and design that reflects you and your personality.

The beads don't need to be used solely for meditation you can use them throughout the day. When you awake hold the beads and run them through your fingers and connect with their energy, this will set you up with positive intentions for the day.

Carry the beads with you in your pocket or bag, take them out during the day to remind you to stay grounded and focus on your tasks; trust me I need these all the time for focusing!

Hold the beads when you feel stressed or spacey to help bring you back centred and calm.

Finish your day the way you started by running the beads through your fingers and counting your blessings. Release the negative points from your day and allow them to be replaced by the positive; feel the good energy from the fabulous points of your day wash over you.

You also don't need to spend huge amounts of money, there are some beautiful meditation beads out there (often called prayer beads or malas), but you can make them yourself with whatever beads you have, there is no need to create a set of beads using expensive natural stones (although they are beautiful and full of natural energy) If all you have are wooden or plastic beads then use them, raid your children's play box even! The idea of the beads is to use them as a focus so even if you have a string of dried peas the intention is the same...

Cake Recipe
This is where you do the work, what is your favourite recipe, what is your favourite thing to eat?

The End and the Beginning...

This is the end of the course, but just the beginning because life, the seasons and the universe works in cycles, never ending, always turning...

Don't stop the course at the end of the twelve months, you have all the materials and knowledge needed to continue working with the energies of each month whether you chose to work with the same goddesses again for the next twelve months or whether you prefer to be open to new ones...the choice and the journey is yours to make.

And finally a huge thank you for joining us on this journey.

We will be here if you need us either via the forum
www.kitchenwitchhearth.net
or on facebook
www.facebook.com/groups/kitchenwitchuk.
You can also email
kitchenwitchhearth@yahoo.com.

Goddess blessings...
Rachel & Tracey

Moon Books invites you to begin or deepen your encounter with
Paganism, in all its rich, creative, flourishing forms.